Kathryn Ochwat
5463 S. Harlan Way
Denver, CO 80123

D0710376

Zen
Gifts
to
Christians

❀

Zen
Gifts
to
Christians

❁

Robert E.
Kennedy

CONTINUUM

NEW YORK ✦ LONDON

The Continuum International Publishing Group Inc
370 Lexington Avenue, New York, NY 10017

The Continuum International Publishing Group Ltd
The Tower Building, 11 York Road, London SE1 7NX

Printed in the United States of America

Library of Congress Cataloging-in-Publication Data

Kennedy, Robert E., 1933–
Zen gifts to Christians / Robert E. Kennedy.
p.   cm.
Includes bibliographical references and index.
ISBN 0-8264-1282-3
1. Kᵒ'-an, 12th cent. Shih niu tᵒ'. 2. Spiritual life—
Zen Buddhism.   3. Spiritual life—Christianity.   I. Title.

BQ9288.K861685 K46 2000
261.2'43—dc21

00-063849

To all my students
with gratitude and admiration,
especially to those who have
become Zen teachers themselves:
Janet Richardson of Baltimore, Maryland,
Ellen and Charles Birx of Radford, Virginia,
and Janet Abels of New York City.

�֍

No greater simplicity exists
than to accept a gift.
John Main

Contents

Author's Acknowledgments

I have had a lot of help in writing this book and many to thank.

First of all I must thank Teresita Fay, RSHM, for her editing, encouragement, and counsel from beginning to end. One of Teresita's many gifts to me in thirty years of friendship is teaching me how to write.

Peggy Greenwood, faculty secretary at Saint Peter's College, typed all these pages, sometimes in her free time. More than anyone else at the college I am indebted to Peggy's patient and professional work.

Rosemary O'Connell helped me with the thankless tasks of assisting with the endnotes, proofreading poetry, and requesting the permission of the poets quoted to use their poetry.

Roy Drake allowed me to use the ox-herding pictures given to him by the Chinese artist Wu Yong Liang, member of the Academy of Fine Arts, Zhzjiang Province, China. Roy's generosity allowed me to give the book the form that it has.

And to my family, Rena and Joe, Marjorie and her late husband Bill, Dorothy and Bill. I am grateful always for a lifetime of love and hospitality.

Publisher's Acknowledgments

Poems 632 and 520 from *The Poems of Emily Dickinson*, ed. Thomas H. Johnson, Cambridge, Mass.: The Belknap Press of Harvard University, copyright © 1951, 1955, 1979 by the President and Fellows of Harvard College. Reprinted by permission of the publishers and Trustees of Amherst College.

"Millennium" © 2000 by Rita Dove. Reprinted by permission of the author.

"After Apple Picking" by Robert Frost, from *The Poetry of Robert Frost*, edited by Edward Connery Lathem, copyright © 1969 by Henry Holt and Company. Reprinted by permission of Henry Holt & Co., LLC.

"Annunciation" by Denise Levertov, from *A Door in the Hive*, © 1989 by Denise Levertov. Reprinted by permission of New Directions Publishing Corp.

"Clouds" by Denise Levertov, from *Poems 1960–1967*, copyright © 1966 by Denise Levertov. Reprinted by permission of New Directions Publishing Corp.

"Contraband" by Denise Levertov, from *Evening Train*, copyright © 1992 by Denise Levertov. Reprinted by permission of New Directions Corp.

"Conversations in Moscow" by Denise Levertov, from *The Freeing of the Dust*, copyright ©1975 by Denise Levertov. Reprinted by permission of New Directions Publishing Corp.

"Empty Hands" by Denise Levertov, from *Sands of the Well*, copyright © 1996 by Denise Levertov. Reprinted by permission of New Directions Publishing Corp.

"One or Two Things," "Orion," "Robert Schuman," "Sun Rise," and "Wild Geese" by Mary *Oliver*, from *Dream Work*, copyright © 1986 by Mary Oliver. Used by permission of Grove/Atlantic, Inc.

"First Snow" by Mary *Oliver*, from *American Primitive* by Mary Oliver, copyright © 1978, 1979, 1980, 1981, 1982, 1983 by Mary Oliver. Used by permission of Little, Bown and Company, Inc.

"Maybe" by Mary *Oliver*, from *House of Light* by Mary Oliver. Copyright © 1990 by Mary Oliver. Reprinted by permission of Beacon Press, Boston.

"White Flowers" and "Rain" by Mary *Oliver*, from *New and Selected Poems* by Mary Oliver, copyright © 1992 by Mary Oliver. Reprinted by permission of Beacon Press, Boston.

"Blue Heron" by Mary Oliver, from *White Pine: Poems and Prose Poems*, copyright © 1994 by May Oliver. Reprinted by permission of Harcourt, Inc.

"Even" by Marie Ponsot, from *The Bird Catcher* by Marie *Ponsot*, copyright © 1998 by Marie Ponsot. Reprinted by permission of Alfred A. Knopf, a Division of Random House.

"The muse of course airs out the inner world," from *Letters from Maine* by May *Sarton*, copyright © 1984 by May Sarton. Used by permission of W. W. Norton & Company, Inc.

"Classifieds" and "An Effort" from *Poems, New and Collected: 1957–1997* by Wislawa *Szymborska*, English translation by Stanislaw Branczak and Clare Cavanagh, copyright © 1998 by Harcourt, Inc., reprinted by permission of the publisher.

"Sky," "Psalm, "A Palaeolithic Fertility Fetish," "View with a Grain of Sand," "No Title Required," "Utopia," and "Nothing Twice" from *View with a Grain of Sand*, copyright 1993 by Wislawa *Szymborska*, English translation by Stanislaw Baranczak and Clare Cavanagh, copyright © 1995 by Harcourt, Inc., reprinted by permission of the publisher.

Introduction

My desire to write this book about Zen gifts to Christians began one morning in 1976 in Kamakura, Japan, where I and some Catholic friends had just completed a five-day period of Zen meditation guided by Yamada Roshi. Standing with them outside the *zendo* (meditation hall), I commented that I was so convinced of the value of the meditation experience when it was guided by the inspirational leadership of Zen teachers that I believed it "belonged in the church."

I became more determined to write this book in 1991 when after fifteen years of practicing Zen, I was installed as a Zen teacher at the recommendation of my teacher Glassman Roshi and his teacher Maezumi Roshi. Their generosity toward me, a Christian and Jesuit priest, reflects the compassionate reaching out toward other faiths which is constitutive of Buddhism and which I believe is present wherever Buddhism flourishes. Indeed, in whatever culture it enters, Buddhism always extends itself to the local religions without losing its own identity.

It is the element of compassionate outreach that inspired me to write this book, title it *Zen Gifts to Christians*, and address it to those Christians who are temperamentally inclined toward practicing Zen to enrich their lives. In no way do I intend to supplant or criticize Christianity. St. Paul tells us that there are many gifts but only one Spirit. And all who attempt to plumb the depths of Christianity know it includes devotional practices for all temperaments. We know that no one devotional practice possesses the whole Christ. We are also aware that when we choose the one practice to which we are most emotionally disposed, we follow it and allow all other practices to fall into its shadow. This is not to say that we deny the worth of the other practices; it simply means that we focus on the form of prayer that encourages us to turn our gaze toward Christ and at the same time to continue to nurture our own particular temperament.

Zen Gifts to Christians is a positive book. Writing it, I hoped to find a place at the Christian table for those whose emotional orientation and Christian faith would be enriched and deepened by the Zen experience. The gifts are practical: that is, they lay down a path of action for us to follow and they offer us a spiritual experience rather than a theory or a theology of religion. They are positive: that is, they add to the worth of the many other gifts that Christianity has received from other traditions throughout time. I especially believe that Zen practice, *zazen* (sitting meditation), and Zen guided meditation will have an extraordinary appeal for contemporary men and women seeking this particular kind of personal spiritual experience. Indeed I have often observed the powerful hold Zen has on the Catholic mind seeking the guided meditation as a form of prayer. Others have witnessed this too. According to Robert Aitken, a Zen master in Hawaii, all the Zen centers in Europe, except for one in France, have been started by Catholics.

Because I believe that Zen must be lived and not just accepted as a concept or theory, this book describes the Zen gifts and shows how we can integrate them into our own lives. It does not teach us how to practice *zazen* (this would be done with an instructor in the *zendo*), but it does attempt to convince us of the importance of *zazen* in helping us make the gifts our own. In it I refer to my own life experience practicing Zen with Zen masters as well as living in and finally directing Zen communities. It is my hope, therefore, that you will not read this book as one more theology of religions, which it is not. Read it rather as a guide to help you understand another form of religious expression and to practice that form if you believe it will develop you spiritually. To begin to understand another form of religious expression is to be open to it, dialogue with those who practice it, recognize and accept the gifts it has to offer.

Perhaps a short summary of how I came to teach Zen and then to write about Zen practice for Christians is appropriate here. Upon my installation as a Zen teacher, after fifteen years of practicing Zen both in Japan and the USA, I set out to teach Zen in my own Catholic community. I was already working as a professor of theology at Saint Peter's College, as a psychotherapist in private practice, and as a priest in neighboring parishes. Almost immediately this Catholic community from neighboring parishes expanded to include ex-Catholics who were no longer interested in further dialogue with the church but who still wanted to attain a greater spiritual depth, which they looked for in Zen. Then came Protestants who were interested in Zen Christian dialogue but not in Zen Catholic dialogue. Following these came Jews who were interested primarily in Zen Jewish compatibility and *zazen*. When shortly thereafter Zen Buddhist students came to my sitting groups, I encouraged them to focus their attention on koans to understand the truths of their own tradition and to become better Zen Buddhists. This was the least I could do to repay my debt to my Zen teachers who labored to make me a better Christian. The diverse interests of the groups inspired me to concentrate on the various aspects of Zen that I believed would contribute to each one's individual development. What the varied groups did for me personally was to broaden and deepen my understanding of interfaith dialogue. Their diversity also enabled and continues to enable me to reach out to people of divergent faith backgrounds who choose to practice Zen to enhance their own devotional orientation.

As our sitting groups became more and more diversified, we did encounter difficulties having to do with traditions and customs and attempts to transplant Japanese customs to American soil. However, because of our ability to dialogue and resolve our conflicts and difficulties, we strengthened our commitment to search for truth together and to continue our fruitful interfaith dialogue.

Today there are a dozen groups of people from many religious persuasions who sit weekly with me in Zen meditation in Connecticut, New Jersey, and New York. Each group has a leader who has his or her own style of leadership and personal emphasis. I encourage individuality as long as it does not lead groups to be so idiosyncratic as to depart from the customs and etiquette that are characteristic of Zen centers worldwide. Besides working with these groups I conduct weekend and week-long *sesshin* (Zen retreats) at various centers in the United States and Mexico.

The extraordinary benefits I have received from practicing and conducting Zen retreats with my diversified groups of students have made me realize that sitting together is a balancing act that bonds us together. It sustains us in our effort to develop our own faith while it allows us to be transformed by the truths of other faiths. I have come to understand what matters most is that we listen to one another, not as adversaries but as compassionate people bringing gifts to one another to help us each discover our still unrecognized possibilities. Surely we do not accept gifts from another religion uncritically but we must accept and reverence gifts from one another molding and integrating them with our own history, tradition, and culture. We must not reject these gifts before we have received, experienced, and understood them in the light of the spirit and culture of the giver.

I view my conducting retreats for Christians and Zen Buddhists as that kind of interfaith work which is a direct and affirmative response to Vatican II and to the thirty-fourth General Congregation of the Society of Jesus. Both concluded that "to be religious today is to be interreligious in a sense that a positive relationship with believers of other faiths is a requirement in a world of religious pluralism."[1] Similarly they both urge us to share with one another our spiritual experiences with regard to prayer, faith, and "ways of searching for God or the Absolute."[2] Already some Jesuits have been trained for this kind of apostolic work. Yet still the Society of Jesus stresses the need for more Jesuits to be involved. It encourages Jesuit superiors to prepare an increasing number of Jesuits and non-Jesuit men and women for interreligious dialogue to understand and appreciate the urgency of this important apostolate in today's pluralistic world.[3]

Sharing our experiences with others, according to the Jesuit general norms, is founded on two important principles. The first principle states that entering into genuine dialogue with believers of other religions requires us to deepen our own Christian faith and commitment, because real interfaith dialogue takes place only between those rooted in their own identity and opened to ongoing development. We do not participate in interfaith dialogue to convert the other to our way of thinking and praying. Instead we take part in this apostolic endeavor to listen attentively to the other in an attitude of respect and admiration at how truth manifests itself differently in other cultures and personalities.

The second principle flows from the first and mandates that we share our religious experience with others. These principles are fostered by Vatican II, which exhorted all Catholics to dialogue with others to "acknowledge, preserve, and promote the spiritual and moral goods found in other religions and the values in their society and culture."[4] This principle moves us into realizing how far we have come from those ages when we went to war with our brothers and sisters of other faiths! Now we are exhorted not merely to tolerate their truth but to promote it. If we are called to promote this truth, then surely we are called to seek it with all our mind and heart and strength.

To enable my readers to comprehend fully the gifts Zen Buddhism has to offer Christians, I have structured this book to follow the process of human development that one undergoes in the practice of Zen Buddhism. This process is depicted in the ox-herding pictures, which date from the twelfth century in China when Master Kakuan drew pictures of ten bulls basing them on earlier Taoist bulls and wrote explanatory comments about each picture in verse.[5] Since then many variations of these pictures have been painted and many verse interpretations have been written. No matter the illustration the ox in the pictures stands for our true nature; the ox herder represents those in search of the truth about their deepest self, and the ten pictures represent the successive steps one must take to realize one's true nature. Both the pictures and the poetry are designed to inspire those who desire to practice the gifts, to become insightful, and to enlist in the compassionate service of others.

In *Zen Gifts to Christians* the protagonist of this poetic picture story, a boy herdsman, stands for none other than you the reader. He is the protagonist of the unique story that is Everyman's, that was born of Everyman's parents and will die on Everyman's deathbed. Inspired, this young herdsman sets out to search for his true self. His quest extends from searching for, to seeing faint traces, to herding, and finally to letting go of the ox. What results is the emergence of his true nature, his return to the source of life: that is, to his whole and complete self.

To explain the meaning of each picture I will present a verse interpretation of it and a koan (case study used to teach Zen students) from one of several classic collections of Zen teachings. The koans for each picture reinforce the picture's specific Zen insight into life. These insights are for me the Zen gifts, which we Christians are already aware of in theory from our own tradition but may not have been sufficiently energized by them to make them a part of our daily living. That is, we may not have perceived these gifts to be as precious and as life-giving as they are. Participating in genuine dialogue with Zen Buddhists or, even better, practicing *zazen* by sitting with complete attention, can help us internalize these gifts. It has been my experience that the disciplined practice of *zazen* can energize us to be present to life with our whole person; it can assist us to become silent and attentive. The practice of *zazen* helps us achieve the spiritual goals that our own Christian doctors of the church inspire us to strive for.

To deepen our understanding of the pictures and to suggest a universal appreciation of the gifts they inspire, I have included poetry and prose from our Western literature. For I believe the authors portray the innate desire of Everyman to embody these gifts. In no way am I posing as a critic of these literary works, nor am I saying the authors practiced Zen Buddhism. I am simply sharing some of their thoughts with you because these thoughts have made the Zen gifts come alive for me. All I wish to convey is that these writers are artists who for me created characters and situations portraying Everyman's search for fulfillment. Many Zen masters, such as Fuketsu and Hakuin, have used art themselves in this way to the great profit of their students. MERTON —

It is my sincere hope that *Zen Gifts to Christians* will delight you as well as give you the insight that will shake your world and contribute to your endless and untiring appreciation of what it means to be a Christian in an interfaith world. I contend that it is our imagination that opens this world to us and urges us to share our gifts with others and to accept gifts from them for the complete joy of us all. What I mean by an imagination that opens an interfaith world to us is best portrayed for me in a poem by the contemporary American poet, Denise Levertov. In it she invites us to:

Imagine this blur of chill, white, gray, vague, sadness
burned off.

Imagine a landscape
of dry clear sunlight, precise shadows,
forms of pure color.

Imagine two neighboring hills, and
your house, my house, looking across, friendly:
imagine ourselves
meeting each other,
bringing gifts, bringing news.

Yes, we need the heat
of imagination's sun
to cut through our bonds of cloud.
And oh, can the great and golden light
warm our flesh that has grown so cold?[6]

Inspired by this beautiful poem let us embark on a journey to genuine interfaith dialogue. Let us throughout this journey share our insights and experiences. And let us learn and grow from the insights and experiences of others. For to do this is indeed a gift, "the pearl of great price."

· I ·

THE SEARCH FOR THE OX

The Gift of Practice

Facing outwards only
the herdsman searches with all his might.
His feet are already in a deep and muddy swamp
but he does not notice.[1]

Let us reflect on what the poet tells us in this verse about the young ox herdsman. We know first of all that he is a beginner because he is "facing outward only" and pursuing a goal other than or even foreign to his very nature. And yet our young beginner has formidable strengths. We know he is well into the practice of searching because his feet are already "in a deep and muddy swamp." He is full of energy and courage and has impressive single-mindedness: he is not preoccupied, in fact, because his attention is so steady, he is totally focused on searching for the ox, which, as I have mentioned earlier, symbolizes our true nature. The verse strongly implies that unless we are totally attentive, unless we search "with all our might," we remain unaware of our true nature. We know that to want to search for the ox is already an awakening of our spirit. This in itself is a precious gift. It is this awakening, this becoming attentive that drives beginning students to start on the long and arduous journey to find and live their true nature. Their journey at this point consists in sitting with great fervor and attention, and listening carefully to the instruction of their teachers.

Zen Buddhists place great emphasis on the importance of attentiveness and practice. Form and teachers play the important role of guiding students and encouraging them to practice "with all their might." The best instruction I have heard for beginners came from Maezumi Roshi in his *zendo* in Los Angeles where I was a student. He told us what I had suspected was true but had not heard so clearly from any teacher before. The roshi said that *zazen* was not only spiritual; it was also mechanical: that is, it was important for us to pay attention to form. He claimed that if we practiced *zazen* correctly, we would in about two years' time receive some insight into our true nature regardless of our spiritual intentions. Maezumi Roshi was so adamant in his insistence that we sit well that he advised us not to sit at all if we were not attentive to form. Actually, one summer afternoon when twenty of us, all Zen students of Maezumi Roshi, were sitting in his *zendo*, he walked in, sniffed the air, and announced that the energy level in the room was too low. He picked up the *keisaku* (stick) used to rouse tired monks and went around the *zendo* striking each one of us. When he put down the stick, he left the room. Indeed as a result our energy level rose and our attentiveness sharpened. We all knew how fortunate we were to have such a teacher.

Zazen is a physical skill and can be compared to any physical skill such as, for example, sailing. There is a correct way to sail that guarantees some success and there is an incorrect way that results in failure. Sailing incorrectly is pitting one muscle carelessly against another; it guarantees only pain and exhaustion. One observant sailor remarked that the sea is not our enemy, but it is unforgiving if we do not sail correctly. In other words, let the would-be sailor beware! So too with *zazen*, let the inattentive sitter beware!

The koan that helped me most to practice *zazen* with attention comes near the end of the book, *The Record of Transmitting the Light*. This koan tells us about the 49th Master who as a young monk listens to his master reflect on a well known teaching which the young monk had often heard before. Hearing it this time, however, he jumps up from his seat and bursts out saying, "Why haven't I heard this before?" We are told he truly heard it at that moment for the first time and became enlightened as a result of his attentive and disciplined sitting. The *teisho* (instruction) the master gives in this koan illustrates the absolute necessity of discipline.

> O monks, if you want to reach this realm in person, you must close your eyes for a while, regulate your breathing, forget your body, have no place to lodge your body, have no need for any relationship with things, become like a cloudless blue sky, and become like the great ocean without waves. Then you will have some experience of it.[2]

Disciplined and attentive sitting empties the mind and prepares it to receive insight into reality. This insistence on the practice of good sitting is shared by all great teachers. Yasutani Roshi, for example, claims that we must throw our whole life into the practice of *zazen*. Teaching his students, he says:

> In the practice of the Buddha way [and in fact it's the same with any "way"] maturity cannot simply be measured in any length of time. There are some who go along lazily, some who make average effort, some who are truly ardent, and some who throw their whole life into it. If they practice for the same amount of time a great difference will emerge in the result, so it can't be measured merely in terms of time.[3]

For his part Master Hakuin, perhaps the most influential Zen teacher in Japan in the last six centuries, compared lazy students to a torn rice bag. He said that no matter how much rice is poured into the top of the bag, nothing is saved, for it spills right out the bottom.[4] So too students who practice fitfully can never hold the energy that *zazen* builds. They will never reach the point of insight that inspired the 49th Master as a young monk to burst out and say, "Why wasn't I told this before?"

Instruction will only teach us how to sit. Finally it is our own practice of sitting, of honing our mechanical/physical skills that will discipline us into attentiveness. Just as the young ox herdsman "searches with all his might" so too in the *zendo* we must learn and practice to sit with complete attention. Of course we all know that for anyone in any walk of life to achieve and master a mechanical/physical skill requires practice and attention. For example, recently I listened to an interview of a professional golfer. An interviewer for TV stopped Greg Norman after he had played brilliantly and had won a major golf tournament. The interviewer asked Norman how he learned to play so well and position his shots so accurately. Perhaps the interviewer expected Norman to speak about his natural gift for the game. Instead Norman replied simply and said that whenever he was not playing in a tournament he made seven hundred practice shots daily. No follow-up question was necessary! No natural gift alone brought Norman to win the prize. Long laborious daily practice of attentively positioning his shots plus the desire to excel empowered him to master the game. So too with Zen practice. Those seekers who go to Japan for training but give up when they first encounter frustration incur the derision of their instructors who call them "three-day boys."

In the spring of 1998 I was privileged to be present at an unforgettable demonstration of attention and practice of mechanical skills at Carnegie Hall in New York City. Anne-Sophie Mutter, a solo violinist, played five sonatas of Beethoven accompanied by Lambert Orkis on the piano. I had never before seen anyone standing alone for two hours playing the violin. I was impressed not only by her genius for music but by her superb athletic posture. She played the violin with her whole body: not just with her fingertips but also with her toes without which she could never have kept her balance and rhythm. No talent in the world could have played so beautifully without having spent years honing the mechanical skills and paying precise attention to the many details of her craft. Her attention to mechanical skills in no way suppressed or minimized her humanity, which was so evident at the very start of the concert. Lambert Orkis, her accompanying pianist, was an elderly man who had difficulty with the tails of his coat as he seated himself at the piano. Anne-Sophie was not too great to put her violin down and assist the old man to be comfortable. Her spontaneous gesture drew an immediate and spirited applause from her sold-out audience.

That attention to technique and to mechanical skills is essential to achieving insight in the theater was the theme of a speech the playwright, Tom Stoppard, gave at the New York Public Library early in 1999. By technique he said he meant the control of information that flows from the play to the audience by hundreds of production cues that adjust the timing, duration, volume, intensity, color, and speed of the play. Stoppard said that we don't like to think of genius employing technique—it almost feels like a contradiction—but the emotional payoff in theater is often handed over to the punctuation of very specific technical cues. Stoppard insisted that theater is a physical event and that the words alone are not enough without everything else. In the extravagant complex equation of sound and light, it is certain words in a certain setting that—often mysteriously—can turn our hearts over.[5] So too in the Zen meditation hall there is enacted among the master, the assistants, and the students, a kind of theater in which many mechanical cues of timing, duration, sound, and light play their part to give structure to aspiration and make it possible—often mysteriously—for our hearts to turn over.

Simone Weil, who has written much on the importance of paying attention, says that our attention is pure only when we are able to attend fully to what is in front of us. This kind of attention is essential to good sitting in the *zendo*. Putting much effort into practicing and listening attentively, students learn to develop increasing control over the obsessive distractions that beset us all. To control distractions, however, does not mean to suppress them. It is futile to try to suppress the mind and even if such a feat were possible, it would create not an attentive mind but a pot of dead ashes. Bodhidharma explains well how to deal with distractions: he says, let the mind circulate freely but let it cling to nothing.

For Weil learning to pay attention includes acknowledging our failures without making excuses for them. Weil explains that by acknowledging our failures we can acquire the virtue of humility, which is a far more precious treasure than all academic achievements. Even the concentration we develop to attain academic achievement is for Weil a tool to form the foundation of our spiritual focus. She writes:

> When we force ourselves to fix the gaze, not only of our eyes but of our souls, upon a school exercise in which we have failed through sheer stupidity, a sense of our mediocrity is borne in upon us with irresistible evidence. If we can arrive at knowing this truth with all our souls we shall be well established on the right foundation.[6]

Especially important to sitting with "the right attention" is Simone Weil's equally convincing advice that twenty minutes of concentrated, untired attention is infinitely better than three hours of frowning application, which serves only to let us say that we have done our duty. Yamada Roshi of Kamakura would agree with her for he always advised us that twenty-five minutes of attentive sitting at one time was sufficient and contended that *zazen* was not an endurance contest to see who could sit the longest. I myself heard him say that exclusive concentration on endurance can turn Zen meditation into "Zen hell."

Although the gift of practice strengthens their ability to pay attention, to stay focused on what they desire, beginning students still need to surrender all barriers that prevent them from finding their true nature. Like the ox herdsman who gives up everything, even his own comfort, they must also give up their old ways and habits to follow the new path their teachers lay out for them.

A recent article on dancing written by Joan Acocella and subtitled "controlled anarchy and self-abandon" clarifies the importance of having good teachers as well as practicing with attention.[7] In this article Acocella insists that most dancers don't develop into anything interesting unless choreographers continue to make new and interesting roles for them. She contends that we don't get a Suzanne Farrell without a George Balanchine, or a Margot Fonteyn without a Frederick Ashton.

Acocella agrees that most young dancers have inherently some special gift that is there from their teens. It's who they are. One has speed, another delicacy, another stage presence. But without challenging experiences their gifts can become repetitious and lifeless. To avoid this from happening, these gifts, according to Acocella, must be bent, even by a sort of "ballet Zen," and must be damped down by a choreographer. When this happens, the dancer works, gives up old habits and cherished strengths to dance into new territory. Acocella singles out Susan Jaffe who, under the direction of Suzanne Farrell, stopped impersonating a Catholic school girl and learned to come alive, heat up, expand, and fill the ballet's skin.

Performing under the direction of a master is not difficult or burdensome. To a true artistic talent the challenge is longed for. Painful and frustrating though the challenge surely is at times, it is sought out and embraced as the sole means to come alive, expand, and fill the gift one initially possessed only as a promise. Similar to the dancers, Zen students under the care of a master must allow their gifts to be bent and damped down. They must give up their cherished strengths in order to move into "new territory." Because serious and dedicated students long for this death and transformation, they embark like the ox herdsman on a path they have never before traveled following signs posted there by others.

Paying attention while allowing oneself to be damped down is a noble and costly goal. It is essential to every aspect of our life. Literature often praises this goal and depicts scenes showing the cost one must pay to achieve and retain it. One scene in particular evokes in us heartbreaking emotions as we watch a young female character unable to exact such discipline of herself. The scene is in George Eliot's novel *Daniel Deronda* and places Gwendolen, a beautiful and once carefree wealthy young woman, in the presence of Herr Klesmer, a focused, attentive, and successful artist. Because Gwendolen's family has recently lost its fortune, she is now forced to earn her living. Naively believing she has talent for the theater, she consults Herr Klesmer about her chances for success as an actress or as a singer in as high-ranking a position as possible. Gwendolen has no doubt that once having made her serious appeal to Klesmer, his judgment toward her will be favorable. She never thinks of the practice and discipline and focus such a goal demands. Filled with compassion for this "undisciplined" girl who all her life until now has only received compliments and praise, Klesmer tells her that to become an artist she must "try the life of arduous, unceasing work, and—uncertain praise." He continues: "Your praise [will] have to be earned, like your bread; and both [will] come slowly, scantily—what do I say? They [may] hardly come at all."[8]

Gwendolen turns from her honest tutor and with an air of pique says:

> I thought you, being an artist, would consider the life one of the most honorable and delightful. And if I can do nothing better?—
> I suppose I can put up with the same risks as other people do.[9]

In spite of his determination to be patient with her ignorant eagerness, Klesmer answers with a little fire:

> No. . . . You could do nothing better—neither man nor woman could do anything better. . . . I am not decrying the life of the true artist. I am exalting it. I say, it is out of the reach of any but—natures framed to love perfection and to labor for it; ready like all true lovers, to endure, to wait, to say I am not yet worthy, but she—Art, my mistress—is worthy, and I will live to merit her.[10]

Because Klesmer fears that he had not penetrated the depths of her soul to help her understand what it takes to be an artist, he tells her that to become one she must unlearn "her insignificant playing at life." And with fervor he adds:

> You have not yet conceived what excellence is: you must unlearn your mistaken admirations. You must know what you have to strive for and then you must subdue your mind and body to unbroken discipline. Your mind, I say. For you must not be thinking of celebrity: — put that candle out of your eyes, and look only at excellence.[11]

What Klesmer is telling Gwendolen is that to become an artist she must "face outwards only" and like the ox herdsman "search with all [her] might," and not "notice" any discomfort. Because of what she has until now been used to — that is, immediate praise for "unworthy" triumphs — Klesmer wonders whether she can search and be content to keep her gaze fixed only on the object of the search instead of on her self-indulgent needs. Klesmer knows that wanting and willing results cannot accomplish them. We must make every effort but we must wait in readiness to accept the results when they come because the object of our endeavor cannot be won by will power alone; waiting and readiness are essential.

The contemporary poet, May Sarton, presents this same insight in a poem she wrote about the absolute giftedness of our achieving the goal of our "search." Effort and will power alone, the poet tells us, are of no avail:

> . . . The Muse
> Ripples the waters, opens doors,
> Lets in sunlight, dazzles and delights. . . .
>
> There is no way to make it happen by will.
> No muse appears when invoked, dire need
> Will not rouse her pity.
>   She comes when she can,
> She too, no doubt, rising from the sea
> Like Aphrodite on her shell when it is time,

When the impersonal tide bears her to the shore
To play a difficult role she has not chosen,
To free a prisoner she has no reason to love.[12]

Besides conforming to the mandate to be always ready, Klesmer tells Gwendolen that an artist must also respond fully to the call to excellence. Zen masters in like manner tell their students that Zen calls them to strive for excellence and shows them how to achieve it. For his part Yamada Roshi of Kamakura would not teach students who did not strive for excellence, who did not seek to enflesh the highest ideals of Zen Buddhism. He often quoted the words of the Pure Land Saint Shinran, "to strive for anything else apart from these ideals, even for enlightenment or teaching status, would be simply shameful."[13]

What does all this talk about discipline, practice, and attention to form have to do with Christian prayer and life? And why should Christian people receive any sort of mechanics (practice) as a gift? For some people mechanics have nothing to do with prayer. These pray as they walk: spontaneously and with all their idiosyncrasies. For many others however some mechanics or method have everything to do with prayer. Without them these people become restless and distracted even at liturgical gatherings. Would not the gift of practice, of being totally attentive, help us to participate more fully in the liturgy and recall the death and resurrection of Christ more vividly? Why would we, who would not play a game of golf without serving some apprenticeship, come into the presence of God's mystery, truth, and revelation with no preparation at all? Do we expect that transformation, death, and resurrection in Christ will happen to us if we cannot even pay attention?

If the "mistress we serve" is God's transforming presence in our lives, then how can we make ourselves "worthy" of her? How shall we labor and wait—that is—be attentive—a lifetime for her? Can the answer to these soul-searching questions be found in this Zen gift? Can disciplined awareness encourage us to pay attention and focus our gaze as we wait for the bridegroom with our lamps filled with oil? If it can, then let us receive and practice this gift from our Zen brothers and sisters with deep gratitude.

· II ·

FINDING TRACES OF THE OX

The Gift of "Not Knowing"

Many look for the ox
but few have ever seen him.
Has the herdsman found him on the north side of
the mountains or on the south?
The one way of light and darkness, along which
each thing goes and comes.
If the herdsman finds himself on such a path
everything is all right.[1]

J ust as the herdsman, so too many set out in search of the ox, the symbol of our true nature. The desire to search and to practice is the first step. The second step is to let go of everything we thought we were certain of. The poet of the verse for this picture tells us that the need to know we are on the right path, or that we are moving toward some fixed truth, will surely hinder us. He tells us that "the one way of light and darkness" is the way that sees no one thing and possesses no one truth. When the herdsman walks on this path of not knowing, the poet assures us "everything is all right."

To be on "the one way of light and darkness, along which everything goes and comes" reminds me of the koan about the 8th Patriarch, Buddhanandi. As a student he approaches his teacher, Vasumitra, and says, "I have come to discuss the truth with you." Vasumitra responds, "Good sir, if you discuss it, it is not the truth; truth is not discussed. If you intend to discuss the truth, then in the end it is not a discussion of truth."[2] Buddhanandi understands what Vasumitra is saying and like the herdsman he sets out on the path of "light and darkness" where all is one: that is, where there is no one truth to be known. In Zen the explanation of this case study is most helpful. It lists a number of true teachings of Buddhism and says that they are not the truth. For example, if we say mind and object are one, this is not the truth. Or if we say mind and object are both forgotten, this is not the truth. Again, if we say that mind and object are not forgotten, this is not the truth. The case study teaches us not to seek the truth in words or in silence. In fact we cannot see the truth even in a dream.

I believe both Jews and Christians can appreciate the care with which Zen Buddhists approach the "truth" and "Everyman's" inability to know it. In Jewish literature and tradition a good example of not holding rigidly to a truth once defined but to keep pursuing its meaning while remaining comfortable in "not knowing" can be seen in John Keenan's book, *The Mystery of Christ*. In it Keenan tells us that:

> Relying on what he had already found, [Abraham] stretched himself forth to the things that were before. . . . And . . . he kept constantly transcending what he had grasped by his own power, for this was inferior to what he sought.[3]

And we Christians too in our Jewish spirit must forget what we have attained and stretch forth *(epektasis)* to what is ahead (Philippians 3:13). For St. Gregory of Nyssa and the fathers of the church the truth of God was not a system of static, self-enclosed stages which led to a state of blessed immobility. Rather it was an unending process in which every attainment was the starting point for yet further progress.[4]

We Christians have devised wonderful philosophies and theologies; we have scriptures and dogmas and truths, some of which we believe to be infallible. We have a centuries' old religious civilization that offers moral and artistic inspiration. Indeed we have much. But if we understand the writings of St. Gregory of Nyssa and other fathers of the church, we realize we do not have the truth, not even in a dream. We realize that we cannot grasp any truth as a finality to which nothing can be added and that this not grasping at truths is the path to human and spiritual development.

It is not only religious thinkers who experience "not knowing" as a life-giving stance. Wislawa Szymborska, the winner of the 1996 Nobel Prize for literature clearly would not have us stuck on a given truth, no matter how sacred. In her introduction to *Poems New and Collected 1957–1997* she writes:

. . . any knowledge that doesn't lead to new questions quickly dies out: it fails to maintain the temperature required for sustaining life. In the most extreme cases . . . it even poses a lethal threat to society. This is why I value that little phrase "I don't know" so highly.[5]

What we think we do know ~

In the same introduction Szymborska writes that all inspiration is born of a continuous "I don't know." This is to be free from the known, to go beyond our comfort zone, and to risk venturing out into the unknown. Writing about people who have become world renown because of their incessant search into the unknown, Szymborska tells us that:

> Had my compatriot Marie Sklodowska-Curie never said to herself "I don't know," she probably would have wound up teaching chemistry at some private high school for young ladies from good families.[6]

But instead of localizing her gifts, Madame Curie, Szymborska reminds us, went on to discover cures benefiting humankind for all ages. However, Szymborska will not let us believe that only scientists must have the talent to go beyond the ordinary. Herself a poet, Szymborska contends that poets must be faithful to their inspiration to move beyond the ordinary. Of these she writes that if they are genuine, they must constantly repeat "I don't know." As soon as a poem is completed and the final period hits the page, she tells us, the poet reviews it only to realize that the particular motif used was pure makeshift, absolutely inadequate. Reading one of Szymborska's poems, we see how she creates images that escape all known and final descriptions, and as a result bring her readers to silence. Take for example her poem "Classifieds" in which she tells us:

> I teach silence
> in all languages
> through intensive examination of:
> The starry sky
> The Sinanthropus' jaws,
> a grasshopper's hop,

an infant's finger nails,
plankton,
a snowflake.[7]

Szymborska goes so far as to say that the land where all truth can be known exists nowhere. In a magnificent poem she shows us that no human being can live on a land where or in a time when absolute truth is known. Significantly, she calls the poem "Utopia" which we know means "nowhere." Let me quote those lines of the poem which reinforce the enormous richness of the Zen gift, "not knowing" so that they will encourage us not to stunt our development by adhering slavishly to *truths*:

Island where all becomes clear

Solid ground beneath your feet.

The only roads are those that offer access.

Bushes bend beneath the weight of proofs.
. . . .

If any doubts arise, the wind dispels them instantly.

Echoes stir unsummoned
And eagerly explain all the secrets of the worlds.

On the right a cave where meaning lies.

On the left the Lake of Deep Conviction.
Truth breaks from the bottom and bobs to the surface.

Unshakable Confidence towers over the valley.
Its peak offers an excellent view of the Essence of Things.

For all its charms, the island is uninhabited,

and the faint footprints scattered on its beaches
turn without exception to the sea.

As if all you can do here is leave
and plunge, never to return, into the depths.

Into unfathomable life.[8]

Other poets too have written about the importance of not believing one owns the whole truth. For example in her poem "Conversation in Moscow," Denise Levertov writes of the vital place silence and the mysterious, which to her are synonymous with "not knowing," have in our lives. The speaker in this poem defines two kinds of poems:

> . . . the poet now
> out of his stillness is talking: "Poems," he says,
> "poems are of two kinds: those with mystery,
>   those without mystery."
> "And are poems without mystery poems at all?" Well . . . yes;
> one cannot say
> a poem well-made, effective, but unmysterious,
> has no value. But for myself—
> I prefer the mysterious . . .[9]

Levertov's speaker "prefer[s] the mysterious" because it teases our mind and disallows us to rest contentedly on any given truth. As such the mysterious calls us to pursue it, letting us know at the same time we will never understand it. For indeed everything to some degree is mysterious, ourselves most of all. And to accept the mysterious is to accept that there is no unchanging truth available to us, that our knowledge is evolutionary and consequently relative. To accept all this can cause frightening disorientation.[10]

To accept the gift of "not knowing" and to admit to ourselves that we do not know God implies risk and a sense of feeling abandoned. For his part the poet Stephen Dunn warns us that the loss of any cherished way of looking at God, any shift in emphasis is painful. When we put aside the certitudes that have upheld us, we always face the risk of total doubt. When he changed his gaze from looking at the known, Dunn writes of the risk he knew he was taking. As if to convince himself to shift, he tells us he talked to himself:

> I'm saying this to myself: the sacred cannot be found unless you give up some old version of it. And when you do, *mon semblable, mon frère*, I swear there'll be an emptiness it'll take a lifetime to fill.[11]

Contemporary Christian writers also reflect on the significance of "not knowing." In his ongoing correspondence discussing prayer and spiritual development with the Polish writer Czeslaw Milosz, we read that Thomas Merton agrees with Milosz and rejects the practice of holding on to "known" truths. To confirm his agreement Merton tells Milosz that we all must step back from our wordy discussions, step back from the ready-made shells of captive positions, "and do God the honor of silence." And later Merton writes:

> As for providence: certainly I think the glib clichés that are made about the will of God are enough to make anyone lose his faith. Such clichés are still possible in America but I don't see how they can still survive in Europe, at least for anyone who has seen a concentration camp. For my part, I have given up my compulsive need to answer such questions neatly. It is safer and cleaner to remain inarticulate, and does more honor to God.[12]

After concurring with Merton on the importance of not looking for neat answers to any of our concerns, Milosz goes a step farther and cautions Merton not to continue to spiritualize or explain nature in his books as if nature were always fixed and somehow synonymous with the truth. To drive his point home Milosz tells Merton:

> I wait for a moment when you meet nature not only in its beauty or calm but also in its immutability of law: a dead beetle on your path.[13]

Milosz tears away every semblance of certainty and would have Merton do the same for himself and his readers.

Another writer who fully grasped the futility of needing to know, of needing to hang on to the truths and customs we know to be lifeless, is Iris Murdoch, the Booker award-winning British novelist and humanist. For Murdoch clinging to known truths is the opposite of paying attention, and paying attention for Murdoch is equivalent to growing up. And we know that both growing up and paying attention are not easily won. For Murdoch they were matters of struggling to perceive the world with less preconception and to understand the provisionality of life-myths, which lead us to repeat roles in emotional systems whose patterns are laid down early in life. In her writings Murdoch tells us that it is the function of art to destroy the cloud of comfortable images with which we surround ourselves in our daily living. She would have us tear down the walls of truth and dogma. "Not knowing" for Murdoch is our capacity to see that we do not really see one another at all, much less do we see God and God's revelation. In *The Green Knight* Murdoch has Father Damien write to Bellamy, a self-absorbed young man, to tell him that he cannot become holy by renouncing worldly pleasures or by looking for signs in scripture or revelations. Instead, to shake him into living in reality and to experience life without indulging in fantasies, even "holy" ones, Father Damien harshly reprimands Bellamy and admonishes him:

> You must not look for revelations or for signs, these are mere selfish thrills which you mistake for adoration, what you take for humility is the charm of masochism, what you call the dark night is the obscurity of the restless soul, by picturing the end of the road you imagine you have reached it, you cherish magic which is the enemy of truth.[14]

For Murdoch "truth" here is "not knowing." It is to keep unraveling our comfort zone until we face the unknowable. In the same letter to Bellamy Father Damien tells him that instead of trying to feel good about himself and thinking he has achieved the truth, which can't be achieved, he should be happy and make others happy, that is your path . . . be quiet, humble, know that what you can achieve is *little*. . . . Pray always, stay at home and do not look for God outside your own soul.[15]

Father Damien's advice to Bellamy reminds us of the experiences of the ox herdsman on his journey to his "true self." Bellamy is not to "face outward." Instead he is to understand that he is the truth he is searching for, and when he understands this, he is to go to the marketplace — as the ox herdsman will eventually do — to "make others happy."

Murdoch's idea of "not knowing" encourages us not to hold on to "bookish" or theoretical knowledge as truth but to live more vibrantly and by our very lives radiate to others our freedom and our commitment to serve them. Also in *The Green Knight* Murdoch describes vividly the three young women who form the core of the novel. To Murdoch they live "at the bottom of a well," which is her way of saying that they are lifeless and live leaden lives bowed down with noble values and crammed with good behavior. To the author the three women are like sleep walkers with no spirit or sexuality, and laden down with too much cold milk. Murdoch stresses that their salvation from this conventional life lies in immediate conversion to welcoming risks and acquiescing in "not knowing," and in finding some regular work to do in the service of others. That is, they should "not sit around all day reading Eckhart" or hopelessly looking for a truth to hide themselves from reality.[16] And to instruct her readers on the importance of "not knowing," three times in the novel Murdoch returns to the advice Virgil gives Dante in the *Purgatorio* before he bids him farewell:

> Do not expect any word or sign from me. Our will is free, upright and sound, it would be wrong not to be ruled by its good sense. And so, master of yourself, I crown you and I mitre you.[17]

Like Merton, Murdoch does not encourage us to wait for signs or revelations, or to weave theories or contemplate values that would have us stand still and risk not growing. Wonderfully Murdoch would have us use the human development gained by our freedom from the known in the service of others. Very much in the spirit of Milosz, Merton, and Murdoch, Wislawa Szymborska in her poem "No Title Required" would have us contemplate life's infinite complexities and come to the conclusion with her about the uncertainty and unimportance of "known truths":

> The tapestry of circumstances is intricate and dense.
> Ants stitching in the grass.
> The grass sewn into the ground.
> The pattern of a wave being needled by a twig.
>
> So it happens that I am and look.
> Above me a white butterfly is fluttering through the air
> on wings that are its alone,
> and a shadow skims through my hands
> that is none other than itself, no one else's but its own.
>
> When I see such things, I'm no longer sure
> that what's important
> is more important than what's not.[18]

Reflecting on this Zen gift of "not knowing," I am reminded of reading in the autobiography of St. Thérèse, the Little Flower, that on her deathbed she suffered the temptation that there was no heaven waiting for her. I believe this is a way of saying she was tempted to think there was no God waiting for her either.[19] These temptations, nevertheless, did not lessen her blind faith. She died "not knowing" but certainly not in despair. Since St. Thérèse is not only a saint but a doctor of the church, we would do well to pay attention to her experience. We must have the faith that goes beyond our "knowing" and let go of our once-cherished truths that no longer obtain. It is faith that demands the destruction of what faith built.

I believe the temptation of St. Thérèse was not a temptation at all; rather it was for her and for all other Christians who enter this "dark night" the natural evolution of the human mind. According to the Benedictine and Zen master, Willigis Jäger, to "not know" and to live

willingly in this state of mind and still continue to pay attention and wait
for God is to grow. He writes:

> It is a decisive step when the individual in contemplation suddenly
> finds . . . God vanishing out of sight, or simply crumbling to pieces.
> This experience can at first give rise to great uncertainty. The
> Father's hand is withdrawn, loneliness and a sense of lostness turn
> into a kind of abyss.[20]

God vanishing from sight has perhaps been felt by many of us even
though we may have lacked the verbal ability to express our sense of loss.
In her poem "Empty Hands" Denise Levertov reflects on the feelings of
abandonment we may have felt:

> In the night foundations crumble.
> God's image was contrived
> of beaten alloy. A thin clatter
> as it tumbles from its niche.
>
> . . . Convictions
>
> wheel and scatter,
> white birds affrighted.
>
> In time you sleep. But wake
> to the same sensation: adrift
> mid-ocean, frayed mooring ropes
> trailing behind you, swirling.
>
> Yet when you open
> unwilling eyes, you see the day
> is sunlit, you walk
> down to the real shore
>
> . . . The past night

remains with you, but your attention
is drawn away from it
to taste the autumn light, falling
into your empty hands.[21]

Not only is the experience of the loss of God common to fervent Christians, I believe it is the experience that Christ himself suffered on the cross. And we know we have still not fully understood his final words: "My God, why have you deserted me?"(Mark 15:34)

Contemplating Christ's last words and the abandonment he suffered, we must remember that the words of the commandment "Thou shalt not put strange gods before me," tell us we are to have no image of God at all. We must discard not only idols but even all conceptions and mental images of God. Does not the Zen gift of "not knowing" reinforce this commandment? We know we can't even say that God is good. Given our limited understanding and language, we can only say what God is not. To help us grasp this truth Keenan quotes Master Eckhart's mandate: "Keep silent and don't gape after God, for by gaping after him, you are lying, you are committing sin." To show us how Eckhart lived his mandate, Keenan tells us that Eckhart begged God to relieve him of a God who was simply the product of his thought and imagination. Such a God, according to Eckhart, would disappear as soon as his thought of God did. And so he counseled that no person should be satisfied in such a God. Keenan then refers to the words of Gregory of Nyssa in *The Life of Moses* to reinforce this message:

> The man who thinks that God can be known does not really have life, for he has been diverted from true being, to something devised by his own imagination.[22]

It is true most Christians do not journey this arduous road of "not knowing" in prayer, but for those who do, Zen meditation can be a great help. For the very purpose of Zen meditation is for us to see into the emptiness of our concepts and emotions as well as into the emptiness of a culture that carries or expresses our faith. Zen reminds us of our own

Christian truth that we need not subscribe to any philosophy or theology or any cultural expression of faith to direct our gaze toward God. Actually Zen's gift to us, to live by "not knowing," serves to help us understand that often it is not belief in God that we lose when our faith is sorely tempted, but belief or interest in the philosophy, theology, or culture that expresses this belief. Again I am reminded of the Little Flower who discontinued reciting the rosary because she did not find it helpful. The rosary here is but a symbol of any form of piety or thought in Christendom. Any cultural expression of faith is itself not faith; let us not cling to mere expressions of faith. Let us realize that to die and rise with Christ is quite enough for any Christian.

By now you may be asking yourself: if Christian thought has long taught us not to cling to any ideas about God, why should we go to Zen Buddhism to learn anew the truths taught to Christians fifteen centuries ago and still very much a part of our Christian tradition? The answer to this question is that to focus on what we learned fifteen centuries ago is not the only goal of Christianity. Rather the goal of Christianity is to move us from a notional understanding of the truth to a vital experience of it in our lives today. I believe interfaith dialogue can help us achieve this goal.

The Zen teaching of Master Vasumitra is a good place to begin our exploration of this gift that Zen lays at our feet to help us achieve the goal of Christianity. Vasumitra would have us learn silence and be comfortable with "not knowing" in order to see the value in the night, and above all, to avoid what Merton calls the clichés about the will of God. Finally Vasumitra would warn us not to seek the ox (our true nature) either in "knowing" or in "not knowing." Rather he would have us experience truth as surely as we do our own parents. And just as we never have to ask who our parents are, so too we should never have to ask others what the truth is—we will experience our truth for ourselves.

In a beautiful poem Wislawa Szymborska, using the metaphor of the sky to signify each person's personal experience of the truth, reflects on how the truth is always with us. Interestingly the poet who is an advocate of "not knowing" never defines the truth. Her message is that truth is always present to us if we are open to accept it in its wholeness and not attempt to dissect it:

I should have begun with this: the sky

. . . .

I don't have to wait for a starry night,
I don't have to crane my neck
to get a look at it.
I've got the sky behind my back, at hand, and on my eyelids.
The sky binds me tight
and sweeps me off my feet.

Even the highest mountains
are no closer to the sky
than the deepest valleys.
There's no more of it in one place
than another . . . .

Division into sky and earth—
it's not the proper way
to contemplate this wholeness.[23]

· III ·

FINDING THE OX

The Gift of Self-Reliance

When the herdsman opens his eyes and takes a look
he sees nothing other than himself.
There is no longer a place for the ox to hide.[1]

T he gift the third picture epitomizes is self-reliance. It is at this stage
of the journey that the ox herdsman realizes that his true nature is within
himself. Here we watch him on his journey in possession of the gifts he
has already received and made his own. He is totally attentive and content with "not knowing." He is ready to receive another important insight.
The verse tells us that he opens his eyes and sees nothing: that is, he
finally experiences the reality that he himself is the ox: the ox is not outside himself and that he must now rely only on himself. This gift of self-
reliance makes him stronger in his determination to live his own true
nature to the fullest extent possible.

The 7th koan of the *Blue Cliff Records* comes to mind as I reflect on
this picture which depicts the real awakening of the herdsman. The koan
is very brief and unforgettable. It tells the story of a monk who approaches
Master Hogen with "My name is Echo. I ask you, what is the Buddha?"
Hogen replies, "You are Echo." It is pure coincidence that the monk's
name, Echo, sounds like the English word "echo." And this coincidence
not only works in our favor but also heightens the drama of the koan as
Master Hogen echoes back the monk's question, "You are Echo," why
do you need to ask about the Buddha? What Hogen is suggesting to Echo
is, "You are the absolute unity of all things. Don't look outside yourself
for anything. The koan tells us that when we realize there is no Buddha
outside the self and when we know we alone are the master, then for the
first time we are worthy to be called "clear-eyed," in other words, self-
reliant.[2] This is the fundamental insight of Zen: nothing exists but the
self and this self contains the whole universe. Another way of saying this
is that there is not a hairsbreadth difference between the seer and the

seen (the herdsman and the ox). To receive the insight that the universe disappears and only the self remains is to understand the absolute unity of all things. This insight makes us self-reliant. Let me quote the verse from the koan that expresses so beautifully what happens to us when we become clear-eyed and self-reliant. It tells us that the whole universe opens up to us and that we are one with it. Nothing is impossible:

> In a moment, peace was restored
> throughout the land;
> All directions lay open
> to the master of the mind.[3]

To be self-reliant, to know that there is no "higher" nature outside the self, relieves the self of the many anxious questions that beset those who rely for salvation on another outside themselves: that is, on a "higher" nature. They are not at peace with themselves and so they fret and fear for themselves. Beginning Zen students who have not yet become self-reliant are often very anxious about their salvation. They often ask, "How many people are saved by the wonderful teachings of Buddhism? Everyone? Many? Few?"

The *Diamond Sutra*, a Buddhist scripture, teaches that "no one will be saved by the wonderful teaching of Buddhism" that is, no one will be saved by something outside the self."[4] This is the understanding that the ox herdsman comes to at this stage of his journey. And like the ox herdsman the first time Zen practitioners perceive that the ox has no place to hide because they and the ox are one, they experience the first moment of insight and see into their true nature. They experience the knowledge that everything they see and experience is none other than themselves.

When I first read about the enlightenment of the Buddha, I was puzzled when he announced that all things were enlightened with him when he was enlightened. I wondered how this could be. But then I finally grasped that not only did the Buddha understand that what he perceived was not a higher nature, he also understood that everything he perceived was none other than himself, and therefore it too was enlightened.

The contemporary American poet Mary Oliver often describes the effects of this insight on the speakers in her poems. In one beautiful poem she captures the speaker at the moment of keen self-awareness. The speaker is caught up in the realization that the self and nature are one. Reliving the experience, the speaker tells us:

> Never in my life
> had I felt myself so near
> that porous line
> where my own body was done with
> and the roots and the stems and the flowers
> began.[5]

It seems as though Oliver is telling us that when we see the world as it is, all division and separateness dissolve. Seeing the world thus makes us self-reliant and we convince ourselves that since there is nothing else but the self what else have we to rely on? The 49th koan of *The Book of Serenity* expands the meaning of self-reliance. This koan teaches us that we should be self-reliant and never be satisfied only to follow the instructions of our teachers. We must grow beyond them. In this koan the author has Master Dongshan presenting a memorial offering before the image of his late teacher. Observing Dongshan do this, a monk asks him for which of his teacher's instructions does he revere him. The master answers that although he was with him, he never received any instruction from his teacher. As a retort the monk asks, "Then why conduct a service for him?" Dongshan's reply to his monk should never be forgotten by either Zen teachers or students. He says, "I do not esteem my late teacher's virtues or his Buddhist teaching; I only value the fact that he didn't explain everything for me." Still not grasping the point of the extraordinary teaching he is receiving, the monk asks again, "You succeeded your late teacher; then do you agree with him or not?" Dongshan replies, "I half agree, half don't agree." The monk continues, "Why don't you completely agree?" Dongshan gives the monk another remarkable answer. "If I completely agreed, then I would be unfaithful to my late teacher's instructions."[6]

Confidence in one's own judgment, ability

What Dongshan is telling the monk is that to be a student does not mean to become an imitator of one's teacher and that teachers must never clone themselves to their students: that is, different sprouts of the same tree (lineage) should not be identical; they should be luxuriant enough to make their spiritual roots dense and firm. The koan especially teaches that "Father and son change and get through" and underlines this wisdom with, "When one's view goes beyond the teacher, then one can handle the transmission." To "go beyond the teacher" does not necessarily mean to be better than the teacher. Such a comparison is not the point of the koan. Rather to "go beyond" in this koan means to stand on one's own feet, to be totally self-reliant so that while grasping one's master's teaching one still owns the personal expression of it. The koan's message is that no Zen teacher should ever demand that a student rigidly conform to the teacher's instruction and no student should ever simply conform to the teacher's directives. That is, adult men and women should never behave in a childish way toward their teachers. Teachers and students should mutually respect one another, be independent, and allow one another's spiritual roots to grow "dense and firm."

To experience the teacher

The Southern American poet James Applewhite illustrates the teaching of the koan in his "Prayer for My Son." In this poem the poet portrays the father's letting go of his son so that his son can follow his own vision and ambition, and be self-reliant. The father describes the scene in which the son leaves the security of his home for New York. Interestingly the father has no desire to venture out from the "slumberous innocence of Bible schools and lemonade," but he can understand the son's wanting to do so. The father tells us:

> . . . My youngest is boarding an airplane
> To a New York he's never seen.
> Raised in such slumberous innocence
> Of Bible schools and lemonade,
> I adjust poorly to this thirst for fame. . . .?

The wise and insightful father prays that his son will "grow into [his] own plumage, brightly" and come to understand that he himself contains all gifts. The father cautions his son that fame comes from within, no matter the city, and that relying on himself the son can attain greatness:

How true

> Oh son,
> Know that the psyche has its own
> Fame, whether known or not, that
> Soul can flame like feathers of a bird.
> Grow into your own plumage, brightly,
> So that any tree is a marvelous city.[7]

What a splendid prayer for a father to hope for his son. He recognizes the more adventurous spirit his young son possesses. In this prayer the father shows himself to be a great teacher. We can hear him advise his son: if you do not achieve recognition for greatness, that is, fame, know that within you fame is born; recognition is not important. Knowing this wherever you are you will know you are in a "marvelous" city.

The importance of self-reliance and venturing beyond one's teacher's counsel is not only the message of the 49th koan in the *Book of Serenity*; it is also the focus of the 41st koan in the same book. In this koan the author tells us that Master Luopu on his deathbed realizes he does not have enough time left to give a long speech. He therefore offers two final statements to his assembled monks: "If you say this is so, this is adding a head to the top of your head. If it is not so, this is cutting off your head." Master Luopu's message is simple and direct. He is telling his monks that if they find that neither of the paths they have been shown will help them develop humanly, they must leave these paths [of yes or no] to find their own path.[8]

In a very interesting poem, Mary Oliver portrays a teacher's thoughts as she reflects on her role as a teacher grooming her students for life. Her speaker is a teacher adamantly defying all "civility" which would have teachers tell their students they are "better than the grass." Listen to the teacher's soliloquy as she proclaims the oneness of all things. The message she conveys in this poem reminds us that if we are all "one," then there are no superiors or inferiors, no controllers or controlled, no worthwhile or worthless. Consequently she breaks down the conventional image we may have of a teacher:

We are one—in spirit—.in creation

. . . And I do not want anymore to be useful, to be docile, to lead
children out of the fields into the text
of civility, to teach them that they are (they are not) better
than the grass.[9]

Not "to lead children out of the fields" recalls life in the garden of
Eden which was certainly not limited by "civility." Similar to the children in the field, Zen students are taught and encouraged to be self-
reliant, to be bold in seeking their own truth. Listen to this exchange in
the koan between Master Luopu and one of his monks. The monk says,
"I don't understand." Luopu says, "You should understand." The monk
says, "I really don't." Luopu shouts, "How miserable." The monk asks,
"What is your meaning?" Luopu says, "The boat of compassion is not
rowed over pure waves: over precipitous straits it is wasted effort to set
out a wooden goose."[10] The phrase "wooden goose," like many Zen say-
ings, seems impenetrable but it is actually quite simple. When coming
to precipitous straits, Chinese sailors on river boats floated a wooden
goose ahead of them to see whether or not it was safe for them to pro-
ceed. Luopu instructs his monks that when finding their own way, they
must not be so cautious as these sailors. They should never rely on the
"wooden goose." They must embrace risks; they must set out, experience
the difficulty, and live through it. And the verse of this koan tranquilly
advises the student that the "precipitous straits" are in reality empty.
Looking outward the student should know that the whole universe is
empty. Instead of the precipitous straits, the student should see that.

> The bait is clouds, the hook the moon, fishing in the clear harbor:
> Old in years, alone at heart, he hasn't got a fish yet
>
> . . .
>
> on the Milo River, the only sober man.[11]

One can easily recognize that "the only sober man" who "hasn't got
a fish yet . . ." can be likened to the ox herdsman. Both open their eyes
and "see nothing other than" themselves; both search and still they wait.
And in their waiting they are attentive, self-reliant; they are not looking
for any one thing.

In a very different tone from the calm and tranquil one that dominates the koan's verse, Rita Dove published her "Millennium Song" on Christmas Day (1999) in the *New York Times*. She too talks of a journey through life. Hers is a festive song depicting an unconcern for what has brought us to the millennium. With joyous exhilaration her speaker tells us she is ready to answer the call to follow whatever it is that "flutters so wildly":

> How do we measure
> this journey—in miles
> or in moments, mistakes
> or monuments? Push off,
> light out, set sail—
> what a festival!
> What fanfare and cheer,
> what a chorus of smiles!
> And there, on the lips
> of the shy, at the tip
> of the world—what is it
> that flutters so wildly,
> a flag or a bird?
> Can you see it? Look,
> look how it flies, how it calls . . .[12]

Do not both the ancient koan's verse and the contemporary poem move us to be aware that all is empty. All is "not knowing," and so we should not cling to illusions. Consequently we must search within ourselves for our true nature and we must do so with confidence and self-reliance.

Similar to the verse of the 41st koan many of the koans include verses that use images to depict not only the insight into the dependent coexistence of all things, but also the self-reliance that flows from this insight. In one koan, to reinforce the importance of self-reliance, the Zen poet uses the image of the carp becoming a dragon, "ascending the falls." Reading the verse reminds us of the beginning of the ox herdsman's search and even more so of his initial awakening and enlightenment. The verse would have us believe that although many desire to search, only the attentive "see" into reality. The many others are the "fools" who "still, by night fish for [the carp] below" not knowing it has ascended the falls and has become a "dragon." The poets tells us:

> Ascending the falls,
> the carp became a dragon
> yet still, by night,
> fools fish for him below.[13]

The ascent of the carp and its transformation into a dragon is a metaphor describing the Zen students' attainment of insight into their own strength and self-reliance. The fools represent those who look to others for support and direction, and never move beyond this stage in their life. They are those who are not comfortable in "not knowing" and so will never become self-reliant. Another image showing the importance of self-reliance in Zen poetry is the tiger commanding his mountain retreat. When the tiger comes to maturity, it attains formidable strength. It becomes a majestic and unapproachable creature that has no need to look for guidance and support beyond itself.

From ancient times Zen literature has abounded in motifs, symbols, and metaphors that function to awake us to the realization of our own potential. Similarly so does the literature of many countries. One especially prominent Irish poet, William Butler Yeats, made it the theme of his visually brilliant poem, "September 1913." Writing in a Catholic country Yeats used images that startle his Christian readers. His purpose in writing was to do just that. He himself, a tireless leader of the Celtic revival and a founder of the Abbey Theatre in Dublin, was a Protestant who took it upon himself to call his countrymen to attention. Although his poem offended many Catholic readers at the time, we read it today as our wake-up call to become less subservient to any form of authority that would suppress our spirit of self-reliance. With its blatant images depicting servitude, Yeats's poem brings to the surface "habits" that deaden the spirit:

> What need you, being come to sense,
> But fumble in a greasy till

And add the halfpence to the pence
And prayer to shivering prayer, until
You have dried the marrow from the bone? . . . *No Hope*
Was it for this the wild geese spread
The grey wing upon every tide.[14]

It seems to me that Yeats is not arguing about the form of prayer so much as about the attitude of the one praying. What kind of person repeats "shivering" prayers that dry "the marrow from the bone"? Contrast that attitude with the self-reliant stance of the "wild geese" who spread their "grey wing[s] upon every tide." Yeats's poem is a plea for his readers to awake, to understand that strength, joy, and purpose come from within the self.

Indeed there are Christians who find comfort in a form of prayer that relies explicitly on the grace and mercy of God for salvation. And yet there are others who because of temperament and life experience agree with and listen to Yeats's call to empowerment. These are self-reliant in prayer, understanding that they themselves are Christ, and "being come to sense" stop begging for favors or forgiveness because they realize that everything has already been given to them and as Zen Buddhists would say "the rice has long been cooked."[15]

In her poem "Wild Geese" Mary Oliver acknowledges that good and evil, guilt and despair, are constituents of the human world. She however would not have us dwell on the potential of evil in life. Instead with Yeats she would have us consider the larger world which calls us to transcend our human worries and to bask in joy, wonder, and self-reliance. She counsels us:

You do not have to be good.
You do not have to walk on your knees
for a hundred miles through the desert, repenting.
You only have to let the soft animal of your body
            love what it loves.
Tell me about despair, yours, and I will tell you mine.
Meanwhile the world goes on.[16]

We don't have to ask for forgiveness of others or of ourselves

in other words don't live in the past — by the past —

And further on in the poem she would, like Yeats again, have us consider the freedom of the wild geese and use our imagination to own our world. With great animation she tells us:

> Meanwhile the wild geese, high in the clear blue air,
> are heading home again.
> Whoever you are, no matter how lonely,
> The world offers itself to your imagination,
> calls to you like the wild geese, harsh and exciting—
> over and over announcing your place
> in the family of things.[17]

Nineteenth and early twentieth century American literature abound in images and metaphors that epitomize self-reliance. Who among us has read Emerson's essay *Self-Reliance*, Thoreau's *Walden* and *Civil Disobedience*, Melville's description of Ishmael in *Moby-Dick*, and Whitman's *Leaves of Grass* without being thrilled at the repeated invitation to stand up and be counted among the self-reliant? They undoubtedly believed that self-reliance is not something external to us but is the salient virtue of our American heritage.

For me, however, perhaps the most poignant example in literature of our need for self-reliance and the tragedy of what can happen to one in whom it has not been nurtured is narrated in Homer's *Odyssey*. The poet moves us with his narration of the return of Odysseus from the Trojan war to his home in Ithaca and to his meeting with his son Telemachus. Throughout the epic whenever referring to Telemachus, Homer uses images depicting a young man in search of a father. When the diffident son recognizes the man his father is, he is terrified. Thinking his father some god, the fearful Telemachus begs only to be spared. Odysseus tries to soothe his son, telling him:

> No, I am not a god . . .
> Why confuse me with one who never dies?
> No, I am your father—
> The Odysseus you wept for all your days,
> you bore the world of pain, the cruel abuse of men.[18]

Another translation of the epic has Odysseus say to his son, "I am the father your boyhood lacked." This version probably helps us to understand better why Telemachus is not self-reliant when Odysseus arrives back from Troy and that he only gradually grows into self-confidence. When Odysseus proposes that the two of them take on the suitors "alone, without allies," Telemachus is filled with fear and asks his father to find others to help them. He cannot yet imagine what two men can accomplish together. But under the tutelage of his father his sense of his own ability and strength grows. We are convinced of his becoming self-reliant when he tells his mother, "The boy you knew is gone." And, to the abusive suitors he boldly announces:

> This is no public place,
> This is Odysseus' house—
> My father won it for me, so it's mine.[19]

And not much later but just before the slaughter of the suitors in the hall, Telemachus acknowledges to his astonished mother:

> As for the bow now,
> men will see to that, but I most of all:
> I hold the reins of power in this house.[20]

Joseph Brodsky writes a modern version of the *Odyssey* in which Odysseus, still journeying home from Troy and not sure of ever reaching it, grieves over how much time he has wasted and how much damage his absence has inflicted on his son. Writing to his son Odysseus advises Telemachus that he has one duty: to grow strong even if he never sees his father again:

> "My dear Telemachus," he writes:
> The Trojan war is over now; I don't recall who won it. . . . But still,
> my homeward way has proved too long. While we were wasting
> time there, old Poseidon, it almost seems, stretched and extended
> space. . . . I can't remember how the war came out; even how old
> you are—I can't remember. . . .[21]

He ends the letter with: "Grow up, then, my Telemachus, grow strong. Only the gods know if we'll see each other again."[22]

If we take this imperative for human growth out of the world of heroic imagination and apply it to our own lives, we can say that at least for some Christians it is not possible to loiter around the altar fearfully pleading for favors or hoping "only to be spared." If we can say anything about "God's will" for us surely it is that we grow to be serene and confident men and women taking our place at our parents' table.

Karl Rahner

your love has hidden itself in silence, so that my love can reveal itself in Faith. You have left me, so that I can discover You. If you were with me, then in my search for You I should always discover only myself. But I must go out of myself, if I am to find You and find You there, where You can be Yourself.

· IV ·

CATCHING THE OX

*The Gift of Accepting Impermanence
and Constant Change*

Grasp the rein harder, do not let go of the ox!

Many, and the most subtle, faults are still not yet overcome.

Even when the herdsman cautiously draws him by the nose with
the rein,

The ox occasionally turns around and wants to go back to the
wilderness.[1]

Return to old ways / comfortable — not accepting change (handwritten marginal note)

In this verse we hear the imperative voice of the poet demanding that the herdsman "grasp the rein harder," so as not to let go of the gifts he has already received and accepted. He will need them to help him from "let[ting] go of the ox." Through the herdsman the poet alerts us to the fact that the more progress we make on our journey, the more arduous it becomes. For, in spite of the herdsman's "cautiously draw[ing] him by the nose with the rein," the ox wants "to go back to the wilderness." In Buddhist terms "to go back to the wilderness" means to turn from the freedom of the Buddha and return to the limitations and clingings of the personal self.

In Christian terms "to go back to the wilderness" is, to use Ivan's words in *The Brothers Karamazov*, to turn our backs on Christ who offers us freedom. Ivan tells his spectators that they are afraid of the freedom Christ offers because it demands that they face and accept reality; that they stop hiding behind their illusions. In classical and psychoanalytic terms "to go back to the wilderness" is dramatized in the *Oresteia* by Aeschylus. In that tragedy to avenge his father's murder, Orestes returns to Thebes to kill his mother. In his modern verse version of this classical tragedy, "The Tower Beyond Tragedy," Robinson Jeffers tells us what happens after Orestes kills his mother. Because Electra wishes to keep her brother forever in the city of Thebes, she offers him the kingdom and her hand in marriage. Orestes refuses this incestuous bonding and tells Electra that he "will not waste inward" and that he must leave Thebes because he "has fallen in love outwards."² If Orestes were to stay with Electra, he would be choosing "to go back to the wilderness," to turn his back on reality.

A Zen gift that can aid us at this milestone of our spiritual journey is the Zen Buddhists' keen perception into reality: that is, their realization and acceptance of the impermanence of all things. This perception allows them to live totally in the present moment which they know to be always in flux. The 13th koan in *The Gateless Gate* is called "Tokusan Carries his Bowls." It demonstrates well the Zen concept of impermanence. Note the emphasis on the present moment in the title. The author tells us that one day the aged abbot, Master Tokusan, comes down to the hall carrying his dinner bowls. A monk sees him and reminds the old abbot that the bell for the noonday meal has not yet sounded. On hearing this Master Tokusan simply turns and walks back to his room. Although some monks laugh at their beloved abbot's forgetfulness, others say the abbot "still does not know the last word in Zen." Actually these latter monks are highly praising their abbot because they realize, as does Master Tokusan, that in an impermanent world such as ours, there can be no last word, no final expression of a truth.

The reality of the present moment in the koan is "it is not yet time for dinner." The wise old man acquiesces. Just as he changes his course from the dining room to return to his room, so too whenever receiving new information, he readily changes his thinking without a hint of defensiveness or denial. Tokusan epitomizes the Zen belief that all teachings are descriptive rather than dogmatic statements. As such they are like rafts, and like rafts they are to be discarded and not carried around once the river has been crossed. This koan ends with a verse in which the speaker cautions us that:

> If you grasp the first word,   ~~START~~
> You will realize the last word.
> The last word and the first word,
> These are not one word.³

This may seem to be no more than a mind teaser; actually it is an experienced reality in Zen Buddhism. There is only the present moment and that is all we have; there is no past or future. Hence the koan's message: neither Tokusan nor any of his monks hear either the first or the last word in life. They accept life's impermanence and the constant flux of all things.

Another koan which illustrates the Zen insight into the impermanence of all things is the 11th koan of *The Book of Serenity*.[4] In it the Zen Master Yumen states that when light does not penetrate freely, two types of sicknesses grow in the dark. The first type of sickness is "not to get on the donkey." Those who suffer from this sickness are those who do not face the reality of the impermanence of all things. Not wanting to stray from their changeless comfort zone, they remain entrenched in anachronistic theories and convictions. They believe the "last word" has been spoken and are therefore not open to change and growth.

Because Zen Buddhism encourages us to go beyond thinking and theory to experience what we think, it teaches that the self is not different from its function of the present moment in this world. The self is simply the sum of its functions at the present moment. This teaching is preventive medicine for the sickness of "not getting on the donkey." Kathleen Raine, a contemporary British poet, dramatizes this "lesson" in a poem in which the action of a gull sharply contrasts the lack of action in a person. Raine contends that only love, that is, only the performing of our role in life, can help us act out our signature, our mission in life. Note the vivid images with which Raine depicts the gull in action and contrast them to the tragic statement: "Man acts amiss"—does nothing!:

> Each creature is the signature of its action.
> The gull swoops, shaped by wind and hunger,
> Eyes and scavenging beak, and strong white wings
> Turned to a fine edge of beauty and power by wind and water.
> Scream and wing-beat utter the holy truth of its being.
> Man acts amiss: pure only the song
> That breaks from the lips of love.[5]

The second type of sickness that grows in the dark where light does not penetrate freely is "not getting off the donkey." This too is a warning to those who cling to the forms and rules of practice even when these forms and rules no longer serve either their purpose or life. One Zen koan that illustrates this sickness tells of a monk, far advanced in training, who comes to a master for further instruction on how to practice and live life.[6] He comes to the master loaded down with Zen scripture, Zen customs, Zen language, Zen clothes; actually he stinks of Zen. The master asks him if he has had his breakfast. "Yes, I have," responds the monk. "Then go wash your bowl," says the Master attempting to convey to the monk that there is no such thing as Zen apart from our very life as we live and practice it moment by moment. The koan warns us not to limit life to scriptures, customs, and theories. Indeed to truly accept impermanence as an aspect of reality we must live freely and not be caught up by forms which no longer serve, even if they once did. For his part, Dogan, a Japanese Zen philosopher of the thirteenth century, cautions us on how to avoid either sickness. He advises us:

> Our body is not really ours. Our life is easily changed by life and circumstances never remaining static. Countless things pass, and we will never see them again. Our mind is also continually changing. Some people wonder, "If this is true on what can we rely?" But others who have the resolve to seek enlightenment, use this constant flux to deepen their enlightenment.[7]

Both sicknesses are sides of the same coin: each side comes from clinging to forms and theories that we have long outgrown. Whether we refuse to get on or off the donkey of "the last word," we stink of Zen. Kathleen Raine would have us understand that for us, as for the phoenix, impermanence is the mysterious process of birth, death, and new birth:

> I am that serpent-haunted cave
> Whose navel breeds the fates of men.
> All wisdom issues from a hole in the earth:
> The gods form in my darkness, and dissolve again.
>
> From my blind womb all Kingdoms come,
> And from my grave seven sleepers prophesy.
> No babe unborn but wakens to my dream,
> No lover but at last entombed in me shall lie.

I am that feared and longed-for burning place
Where man and phoenix are consumed away,
And from my polluted bed arise
New sons, new suns, new skies.[8]

The earth, the "I" of the poem, gives birth to all from "blind" woman to man, birds, kingdoms, gods, wisdom, and the like, according to her wishes and needs. She demands the death of all; and from that death comes "new sons, new suns, new skies." Kathleen Raine has the earth inform us it is at one and the same time the "feared" and "longed-for burning place"; is it "longed for" as a means to end impermanence? We know that out of this "feared and longed-for burning place" "arise new sons, new suns, new skies." Impermanence brings newness, uniqueness. The earth is telling us that there are no standards; we are not to convert impermanence into finality. Instead we are to see the uniqueness in each moment, in each person.

In much the same spirit the 27th koan in *The Record of Transmitting the Light* teaches us how to respond to the uniqueness as well as to the impermanence of all things. The author tells us that Master Panyamitra travels to eastern India to liberate all beings. Because he has planned no set way to liberate the multitudes "in one fell swoop," he promises to liberate each being according to its type, its uniqueness![9] Zen's tolerance of and acceptance for all individual needs helps people develop according to their uniqueness at every given moment of their reality. Writers too tell us how we experience life differently and uniquely at the various stages of life in keeping with our unique needs. Shakespeare for example traces the seven human stages physically from birth to very old age, and tells of the unique characteristics of each age.

Interestingly Ronald Goodman, a contemporary poet, sums up our ever-changing and impermanent uniqueness by assigning dwelling houses for our ever-changing attitudes. In the fourth house Goodman says God is atheos or God is experienced as notexisting. In the third house God is theos, experienced as existent but hidden in nature or hidden in the community as a whole. In the second house God is entheos, experienced in the other, indwelling in each individual. In the first house God is pantheos, experienced as other but now there is only the other, the I-thou division is gone. Because of our uniqueness and our proneness to change, Goodman tells us that at various stages we inhabit different houses. Some of us have rooms in more than one house. Each of us exudes unique house characteristics: ambition, domesticity, searching, gratitude, and these are always in flux. Knowing this, we recognize that in life there is no finality about us; we are one and the same with impermanence.[10]

Writing a poem about the topic of impermanence and the uniqueness that springs from it, Mary Oliver pictures God speaking to us differently each time God approaches us. God conditions the divine voice to our needs, and so we at any given time can say:

> The god of dirt
> came up to me many times and said
> so many wise and delectable things, I lay
> on the grass listening
> to his dog voice,
> crow voice,
> frog voice; *now,*
> he said, and *now,*

and never once mentioned *forever.*[11]

No matter the voice God uses, the poet would have us understand that God's voice is heard _now: _that is, God speaks to us as we are and what we experience at the very moment of God's approach. Oliver would have us understand that impermanence is the fact of life. Similar to Master Tokusan, who carries his bowls, we must be open to the present moment. Only then will we "hear his voice."

Because Zen would have us be aware of the impermanence of all things, Zen teachers always impress upon us the many changes that have taken place in Zen Buddhism itself. It does not proclaim that it always was as it is now. Rather it confesses to change and adapts to the present moment and place wherever it is practiced. For his part, Maezumi Roshi contended that not only does Buddhism change fundamentally, but it must change fundamentally. Shortly before he died Maezumi Roshi claimed that in every century and in every culture that it enters Zen Buddhism must find new forms to teach those people eager to learn about it. It must do this to enable its followers to live deeply in the here and now of their lives. To Maezumi it was unthinkable to have a static Buddhism in an ever-changing world. It was unthinkable for Buddhism to imitate old forms of teaching and living, no matter how precious those forms once may have been.[12]

The impermanence of the moment and its inability to be the "last word," or the revered totality of all is seen in many great works of art. Samuel Beckett, the Irish playwright, is a supreme example. Beckett never thought a play complete when he finished writing the script. Whereas most plays invite the active participation of directors and actors and designers to determine the meaning of the work, Beckett's plays demand the active participation of the audience as well. And because of this, his plays have eluded the very possibility of having a single definitive text. For Beckett the essential act of authorship was not just the writing of a play, but the actual acting out of the work on stage. According to Beckett the written text was a mere schema; the work of art was the production. Beckett knew that the nuances, which are so much a part of all theatrical art, come from the audience as well. Knowing that audiences vary from night to night, Beckett wrote his plays to be open-ended. He wanted no "last word" for any of his plays for fear that they would be merely reproduced again and again, and finally become set pieces with no message or purpose. Actually in *Waiting for Godot* he voices his horror at the evils of automatic repetition and calls them dead habits.

Writing about Beckett's plays, Fintan O'Toole quotes directions that Beckett gave to directors he trusted, saying that "no final script is possible until I have worked on rehearsals." When Beckett was not present at rehearsals, he gave trusted directors freedom to find their own solutions to staging problems and to direct the play their own way. In 1963 the playwright wrote to Alan Schneider, who was preparing for the first American production of *Play*, telling him,

What matters is that you feel the spirit of the thing and the intention as you do. Give them that as best you can, even if it involves certain deviations from what I have written and said.[13]

Beckett trusted Schneider to "feel the spirit" of the play because Schneider had an imagination borne of suffering. He could feel. A Russian Jew raised in Rostov in the midst of civil war and nephew to an aunt who died at Auschwitz, Schneider had experienced firsthand the horrors of the twentieth century. Such a man, Beckett felt, was more to be trusted directing his work than one who slavishly followed a written text. For Schneider, too, there was "no last word" to a play or to life. Schneider could express to the audience what Beckett wanted. He could "make them feel the spirit of suffering and survival in our times."

In American literature, too, we read excerpts that call to mind the impermanence of life and our responsibility to consciously accept it. In Frost's poem "After Apple Picking," the speaker tells us about his lifelong ideal to bring in the harvest, to pick the last two or three apples from every bough. What the speaker desires and envisions is to achieve perfect totality or finality. Fatigue puts him in a dreamworld in which he, like Tokusan before him, realizes that his ideal, his need for totality or the "last word" is not achievable:

> For I have had too much
> Of apple-picking: I am overtired
> Of the great harvest I myself desired.[14]

The speaker realizes that he has tried too hard and long to bring in the harvest he himself so desired to gather; a deeper wisdom tells him to put down his too life-consuming labor ("the last word"), because final perfection and total completion is not part of the human condition. He concludes his soliloquy very ambiguously—will only death bring totality? We know in death "now" becomes "forever." In life there is no forever:

> One can see what will trouble
> This sleep of mine, whatever sleep it is.
> Were he not gone,

The woodchuck could say whether it's like his
Long sleep, as I describe its coming on,
Or just some human sleep.[15]

I believe the Zen teaching concerning "no last word" is a gift to Christians because it helps to open for us a larger and legitimate understanding of the impermanence of all teachings. This in itself fosters interfaith dialogue: We realize that all faiths have a vision they would like to share. We learn to listen without prejudice and without dominating the dialogue. Let us look at current Catholic attitudes toward dialogue as they were manifested in Rome in October 1999 at the Vatican-sponsored summit of the spiritual leaders from various world religions. The Nigerian Cardinal, Francis Arinze, head of the Pontifical Council for Interreligious Dialogue, made three statements, two of which were aimed to help the spiritual leaders not only to avoid controversy but also to find a foundation on which they could all dialogue.

In his first statement to them Arinze stressed that the delegates from the world religions "leave aside speculative discussion." This was a very wise admonition! Since many of the spiritual leaders today are not trained theologians or philosophers, they are not necessarily equipped for or interested in speculative discussions. Moreover their gifts for teaching, healing, and community building need not include proficiency in speculative thought. Furthermore because religious speculative thought is at times simply speculation, it may be carried on without the backing of sound religious experience.

Of the same mind as Arinze, Rosemary Radford Ruether points out that speculative religious discussions can lead to arguments and even to violence as each person believes he or she has the best theory. She contends that it is not unheard of that interfaith meetings break down in anger over differing versions of peace.[16] And let us remember the petition of the disciples of Jesus, "Lord, teach us to pray." They were asking for an experience, not a theory of prayer.

In his second statement on interfaith dialogue, Arinze contended that listening was the "prime objective" of the interfaith summit. Because Bishop Michael Fitzgerald, secretary of the Council for Interreligious

Dialogue, explained what listening meant we should view Arinze's statement in the light of Fitzgerald's thought:

> We have to be concerned with the whole of humanity, thus includ-
> ing people of different religious beliefs. We have to acknowledge
> one another, respect one another and live peacefully together.
> That's what this [summit] is all about.[17]

Arinze's two statements on interfaith dialogue actually clarify my understanding of the Zen insight into the impermanence of all things: no last
word. They also express well how this Zen gift, no last word, is so suit-
able a practice for interfaith meetings. And if this Zen gift were not available to us, we would have to invent something very much like it to satisfy
the participants of interfaith meetings. And this for two reasons: first, the
Zen gift plunges us directly into experience and rejects all speculation
about that which we can never agree on. Practitioners do not pray together;
they only sit attentively together. While this is a necessary pedagogue to
prayer, it need not be called prayer at all. Second, Zen asks us precisely
to listen to everything and everyone: to our neighbors, to their breathing, to their fears, and to their deepest aspirations.

Mary Oliver reminds us that clinging to either the first or the last word
causes immense suffering and isolation:

> Sweet Jesus, talking
> his melancholy madness,
>   stood up in the boat
>   and the sea lay down,
>
> silky and sorry.
> So everybody was saved
>   that night.[18]

In contrast to the sea that "lay down/silky and sorry" when Jesus "talking his melancholy madness" stood up, we walk away from one another
at the slightest hint of conflict. Not knowing our own soul, we cannot
listen to others.

. . . But you know how it is

when something
    different crosses
        the threshold—the uncles
            mutter together,

the women walk away,
    the young brother begins
        to sharpen his knife.
            Nobody knows what the soul is.[19]

· V ·

TAMING THE OX

The Gift of Self-Mastery

The herdsman must not for a moment drop whip or rein,
Or else the ox would stampede into the dust.
But if the ox is patiently tamed and gentled
He will follow the herdsman by himself.[1]

Our poet tells the ox herder that he must tame the ox so that he will not "stampede into the dust" and run wild. The taming must be thorough and lifelong so that the ox, once made gentle, will "follow the herdsman by himself." To be tamed and made gentle, to be patient and steadfast in difficulties, to follow the way by ourselves is to possess the gift of self-mastery. The gift of self-mastery is one that Christians may feel we can appreciate and practice without any help from Zen Buddhism, but it is a gift to see how Zen expresses self-mastery in its own tradition. The Zen practice of self-mastery is expressed in a memorable way in the 9th koan of the *Blue Cliff Records*, "The Four Gates of Master Joshu."[2] In it a monk asks Joshu, "What is Joshu?" Joshu answers, "The East Gate, the West Gate, the North Gate, the South Gate." Joshu's answer is a play on words because he was named after the town of Joshu which has four gates that open to anyone who wants to go in or out. Men and women, young and old, dogs and cattle—all can pass through them. For Joshu himself there are also four gates, symbols of all points of the compass or all aspects of reality. Joshu's self-mastery is so total that all his gates are always thrown open confidently to receive the world.

Because Zen Buddhist masters wanted to guide their students away from what would not lead them to self-mastery, they often referred to three koans in *The Record of Transmitting the Light*, which indicate what self-mastery is not: it is not imitation of another or excessive piety or sacrifice, all of which detract us from developing self-mastery. The first of these koans warns against imitation and it concerns Master Ha of India.[3] He is named Ha after a crane because wherever he goes, a flock of cranes follows him. This Ha asks his master why the birds keep following him. His master replies that in a former lifetime, Ha was a virtuous man and because of his true virtue, he was reborn as a human being. However in that previous lifetime Ha had five hundred disciples who were deluded by the desire to follow an illustrious teacher. As a result, they neglected to develop themselves humanly; therefore they were reborn as birds and they actually still follow Ha in his present lifetime to this very day.

We may wonder why these five hundred devoted disciples were turned into birds for following the example of their gifted master who showed them the way to liberation and the extinction of suffering. The answer is because they remained followers; they never became liberated. We can look upon this koan as a gift and as a warning to avoid imitation; to avoid being only followers, for even if we follow perfectly every word and gesture of a perfect master, it is not enough to bring about our own liberation and development as human beings. In fact should we become perfect followers of the letter of the law, even to the point of imitating another's spirit of the law, we may still be reborn as a flock of birds, because we will not have developed our human potential. What happens to persons who imitate another or look to another to guide their behavior is poignantly presented by Anne Wroe in her biography of Pontius Pilate. Wroe writes that because Pilate had talent and opportunity, he:

> could [have taken] untravelled roads, open[ed] hidden doors, escape[d] the bounds of earth and flesh, exceed[ed] himself. Or he could [have stayed] as he was: shrug, scratch his ear, write another memorandum.[4]

For his part Frank Kermode sees Wroe's Pilate as a worried administrator, petrified of his superiors, and uneasy in dealing with the Jews. He had a chance to be very good, but in his fear he looked to others and did what he thought they wanted.[5] In short, he played it safe and stayed as he was: an imitator, a follower, no different from the birds that followed master Ha.

If imitation is not the way to achieve self-mastery, neither is excessive piety. The second koan is about Master Vasubandhu of India and contains the "greatest secret for learning the way."[6] The author tells us that Vasubandhu becomes a monk at age fifteen and before long becomes the leader of a group of young zealots who value only debate. Besides being over pious he is also a great ascetic: he eats only one meal a day; he never lies down to rest. Day and night he pays reverence to the Buddha; he is pure and desireless, and much admired by his friends and disciples. Fortunately for him the Venerable Jayata comes on the scene and is moved with compassion for the boy and desires to liberate him from his piety. Hearing of Jayata's intention Vasubandhu's alarmed disciples ask Venerable Jayata how he can speak of liberating their pious teacher. "Your teacher is far from the way," responds the Venerable Jayata. "Even if he practices asceticism for countless ages, they (these pious practices) are the roots of vanity and falseness." "Well, what virtue have you accumulated that enables you to slander our teacher?" ask the angry young disciples. Jayata warns them again, "Even if you and your master spend countless ages in ascetical practices, you will not find liberation. These practices are meaningless, they are really a big laugh." "How then are we to be liberated?" the disciples ask. Jayata's answer goes to the heart of self-mastery in Zen Buddhism:

> I do not seek the Way, yet I am not confused.
> I do not venerate the Buddhas, yet I am not conceited.
> I do not meditate for long periods of time, yet I am not lazy.
> I do not restrict myself to just one meal a day, yet I am not attached to food.
> I do not know what is enough, yet I am not covetous.
> When the mind seeks nothing, this is called the Way.[7]

Jayata then goes on to tell the disciples what self-mastery is. He tells them that when their minds seek nothing, when they do not go to ascetical extremes, when they are not attached to what the culture calls pious and proper, and when they do not seek liberation in any external code of rules, then they will reach a realm of happiness and be like people who have eaten their fill. And though they hear of a royal feast elsewhere, they will not be interested in attending it. Self-mastery then is living a full life in the present, attached to nothing.

If self-mastery cannot be reduced to imitation or piety, neither can it be reduced to sacrifice. The third koan tells us about the 35th Patriarch, Wu-chi who lives in an area where the inhabitants are terrified of demons and ghosts. To appease these demons they build shrines where they slaughter cattle as sacrifices.[8] Wu-chi hastens to these shrines and demolishes them and frees the cattle. Doing this Wu-chi liberates not only the cattle but also the people who have been living in ignorance and terror seeking liberation from their fears by sacrificing animals. Perhaps the koan would have us delve to a deeper level than Wu-chi's liberating the cattle. The cattle can stand for the nonrational aspect of our own nature, which Zen would not have us suppress by arbitrary rules of conduct but rather have us liberate and integrate it into a mature and vibrant life. Even more so the cattle can stand for the dark side of our humanity, which Zen would have us understand and accept and reshape through constant practice.

That the way to self-mastery is not to sacrifice our animal energies but to integrate them into a vibrant human life was the constant refrain in the writings of the playwright Anton Chekhov. In a letter to his brother Nikolai, Chekhov urges him to "never stop reading, [never stop] studying in depth, [never stop] exercising [his] will for every hour is precious."[9]

The sacrifice of human talent would be the last thing on Chekhov's mind. Self-mastery for him was not to waste life. In his plays characters reject "tags and labels" and possess the gift of "unfinalizability." They express their freedom through their capacity to surprise. A vulgar, cynical, government clerk, for example, surprises us when he sits down at a piano and plays with astonishing depth and nobility of feeling. Reading Chekhov we are reminded that self-mastery does not exclude frailty and that to attain self-mastery is a lifelong quest. "Life," Chekhov writes, "is given only once and one wants to live it boldly, with full consciousness and beauty." He continuously advises us that it is never too late to reshape our life. In a letter to an editor, speaking about himself, Chekhov writes:

> I am neither liberal nor conservative, nor gradualist, nor monk, nor indifferentist. I would like to be a free artist and nothing else.
> . . . I look upon tags and labels as prejudices. My holy of holies is

the human body, health, intelligence, talent, inspiration, love and
. . . freedom from violence and lies, no matter what form the latter two take.[10]

The "tags and labels" Chekhov rejects include romantic and religious
tags, and labels that can blind us to the beauty and the rich potential of
the world we live in. Even nihilism for Chekhov was simply a "tag." What
Chekhov feared more than nihilism—which is only a theory—was a
wasted life. Referring to his own plays, he writes to an editor:

> You can't end (a play) with the nihilists. . . . If your heroine . . .
> comes to realize that the people around her are idle, useless, and
> wicked people . . . and that she's let life pass her by . . . isn't that
> more frightening than nihilism?[11]

For Chekhov, the sacrifice of human energy and talent is anathema, the
very opposite to self-mastery. It is an irretrievable tragedy.

Self-mastery then from the Zen perspective is the act of confidently
throwing open the gates of our mind and heart to know our own gifts and
talents, and to feel our own power. Think of Mozart, for example, who
grew from a musician of enormous competence in 1782 to an incom-
parable master in 1788 at which time he broke all the rules he had learned
in order to compose his Mass in C Minor. We know he practiced intently
but even so without understanding and mastering the gratuitous gift of
talent he could never have achieved what he did. Think of Walt Whitman
whose writing advanced from the prose of *Franklin Evans* to the poetic
greatness of "Songs of Myself". It was genius and self-mastery that led
him to celebrate life in such an exuberant manner.

It is self-mastery that will enhance the spiritual lives of men and women
today, and then empower them to avoid relying on a self-constructed
image of God. In her essay on contemporary religious life, theologian
Sandra Schneiders writes that modern psychology has made us "brutally"
aware of the powerful role that projection of need plays in the construction
of the God-image:

This God . . . tells us what to do without ambiguity and rewards our self-alienating submission with immortality. He protects us from harm and injustice and keeps our religious persona intact. He makes us special by calling us to a higher life. In short, he is a God made in our image and according to our needs. . . . The theology of our youth connived with our lack of psychological sophistication to keep us spiritually immature.[12]

In the Zen tradition there is a wonderful example of self-mastery in the life of the Buddhist nun, Rengetsu, who lived in the nineteenth century. Thirty-three years old in 1824 and twice widowed, Rengetsu took her vows as a nun. Well-educated and trained in the arts, Rengetsu continued to lead an active life and settled on pottery-making as a means of livelihood. She embellished her pottery with her own poetry written in her unique and elegant calligraphy, distinctively feminine yet strong and supple enough to win the highest praise of the male calligraphers of her generation. She remained productive until the very end of her long life in 1875, producing more than fifty thousand pieces of art. Let me offer two of her poems that advise aspiring Zen students how to attain self-mastery.

One poem is "Dharma Light":

> If you want to
> Extend the light
> Of the Dharma,
> Let it first illumine
> Your own heart.[13]

The second poem reflects her desire for all beginners setting out on their spiritual journey to attain self-mastery, "Seeing Young Nuns on Their Begging Rounds":

> First steps on the
> Long path to Truth:
> Please do not dream

Your lives away,
Walk on to the end.[14]

Zen would delight in St. Luke's Gospel account of the self-mastery of Mary who as a young woman utterly opens wide to God the gates of her mind, heart, and soul. Denise Levertov turns this story into a poem called "Annunciation in the House."

> We know the scene; . . .
>   Arrived on solemn grandeur of great wings,
> the angelic ambassador, standing or hovering,
> whom she acknowledges, a guest.
>
> But we are told of meek obedience. No one mentions
> courage.
>   The engendering Spirit
> did not enter her without consent.
>   God waited.
>
> She was free
> to accept or to refuse, choice
> integral to humanness. . . .
>
> This was the minute no one speaks of,
> when she could still refuse.
>
> A breath unbreathed,
>   Spirit,
>   suspended,
>   waiting.
>
> ---
>
> She did not cry, 'I cannot, I am not worthy,'
> nor, 'I have not the strength.'
> She did not submit with gritted teeth,
>   raging, coerced.

Bravest of all humans,
        consent illumined her. . . .
Consent,
        courage unparalleled,
opened her utterly.

Levertov then questions us, her readers, about our own capacity to be open. She ends her poem on a tragic note for those of us who say we are not worthy and have not the strength to say yes.

Aren't there annunciations
of one sort or another
in most lives?
        Some unwillingly
undertake great destinies,
enact them in sullen pride,
uncomprehending.
        More often
these moments
        when roads of light and storm
        open from darkness in a man or woman,
are turned away from
in dread, in a wave of weakness, in despair
and with relief.
Ordinary lives continue.
        God does not smite them.
But the gates close, the pathway vanishes.[15]

· VI ·

RIDING HOME ON THE
BACK OF THE OX

The Gift of Incarnation

Slowly and steadily the herdsman rides home on the ox.

In the spreading evening mist his flute sounds far into the distance.

Beat by beat and verse by verse the boundless feeling of the herdsman rings out.

Listening to this song there is no need to say how things are with the herdsman.[1]

By the Zen gift of incarnation I mean the total experience of the absolute incarnate in the relative. And although in Zen the absolute and the relative can be distinguished from each other, they cannot be separated. In the sixth ox-herding picture the herdsman experiences totally his (relative) unity with the ox (absolute). Enlightened he rides home in peace: "Slowly and steadily." The sound of the verse is soothing and it reinforces the "boundless feeling of the herdsman." "Listening to [his] song" we intuit how totally at one he is with the ox. *Complete*

Because the experience of the unity between the absolute and the relative is fundamental to Zen Buddhism, it is no surprise that many koans deal with it. The very first koan in *The Record of Transmitting the Light*, for example, relates the account of the enlightenment of the Buddha. It tells us that one morning upon seeing the morning star Sakyamuni Buddha is immediately enlightened. In his joy at this great insight he cries out "I and the great earth and beings simultaneously achieve the way."[2] He exults in his realization that he and the great earth and the whole cosmos and everything in it simultaneously achieve enlightenment; he realizes that they all share the same reality. It was this experience that launched Zen Buddhism as an international religion of wisdom and compassion.

The "I" of this koan, according to the Zen Buddhists, is of course not the man Sakyamuni Buddha; yet he is one with this "I." And going a step further they also teach us that there is no Sakyamuni Buddha apart from the "I" and no part of the "I" that is not Sakyamuni Buddha. Accordingly to say Sakyamuni Buddha becomes enlightened with the earth or with anyone or anything else is not correct, for that would signify separateness; and to say that two separate points of view are similar implies a dualism, which is very different from the meaning of this koan. Instead the koan teaches us that the Buddha, the world, you, and I are neither identical nor different. We are one. This is beautifully expressed in the verse that concludes this koan:

> A splendid branch issues forth from the old plum tree;
> In time, obstructing thorns flourish everywhere.[3]

The lesson we learn is that the "splendid branch," the "old plum tree," and the "obstructing thorns" are one and the same reality, even though we can distinguish them physically from one another.

Having experienced the Zen belief in the unity of the absolute and the relative, Yamada Roshi of Kamakura once told us that he could believe in God. What he could not believe was that God could make a dualistic world. So steeped in the unity of all things, so at one with this world, Yamada Roshi could not imagine a world of separate realities. The roshi did not teach that Sakyamuni became enlightened with him or that he became enlightened with Sakyamuni. Rather he taught that there was no Sakyamuni and no Yamada apart from the phenomena of this world. They were neither identical to nor different from each other. They were one. We ask ourselves, why ever would it be necessary for Yamada Roshi to have to believe that God would or could create a dualistic world? Why would Christians of all people, who believe that God is a Trinity, that is, Three Persons in one reality, present their faith in a dualistic fashion? We believe we are made in the image of God; we know we are one with God, not identical but not separate. How can we believe God created us in God's own image if God can in any way be separate from us? We do not believe that God is only in heaven and we are on earth, and that we relate to God as one who is outside ourselves. Instead, believing that the world is a manifestation of God, we know that the unity of God and the world as well as the unity we have with one another are analogous to the unity of the Three Persons in the Trinity.

Although our Christian faith is nondualistic, our Christian prayers and poetry sometimes appear to be so. Jesus himself told us to pray to our Father who is in heaven. Obeying his mandate it is conceivable that we create an image of the Father; yet we know with full certainty that even in its crudest form, our image will do us no harm. We certainly agree with C.S. Lewis who questioned: "What soul ever perished for believing that God the Father has a beard?"⁴ What we must never think is that our image of a Father in heaven is a concession to our weakness and that only an imageless prayer is the literal truth. Both are concessions and misleading, and the two together are mutually corrective and beyond image and nonimage. But for those Christians drawn to imageless prayer, who sense a reality more intimate than the relation of father to son, or mother to child, or husband to wife, Zen's gift of the incarnation: the unity of the absolute and the relative, can help us understand more fully that God's life is our own: God sees with our eyes; God listens with our hearts. Indeed this gift of incarnation helps us to see that everything shines with the light of Christ who is everything visible about the Father.

Another koan that deals with the sense of unity that the herdsman feels with the ox and which expands to include the unity of all reality is the 17th koan in *The Book of Serenity*. It is called Master Fayan's "Hairsbreadth." In it Fayan in dialogue with a monk says, "A hairsbreadth difference is as the distance between heaven and earth—how do you understand [this]?"

The monk answers, "A hairsbreadth difference is as the distance between heaven and earth."

Fayan asks, "How can you get it that way?"

The monk answers, "I am just thus—what about you?"

Fayan replies, "A hairsbreadth difference is as the distance between heaven and earth."⁵

Fayan means there is not even a hairsbreadth difference between heaven and earth because if there were heaven and earth could never be united and that there is no absolute apart from the relative. All the separate objects of our perception and thought are like flowers in the sky. They have no independent existences of their own; they are one with the eye that sees them.⁶

The author of the koan then invites us to look at the background behind the two conversing monks to watch a pair of solitary wild geese flap on the ground and then fly up high. We are also directed to watch a couple of mandarin ducks that stand alone by the bank of the pond. Pondering the scene, we remember the verse portraying the oneness of the "splendid branch," "the old plum tree," and the "obstructing thorns," and we grasp that similar to them, these geese and ducks and monks are neither identical nor different. Each is a distinct picture of the absolute present in the relative, which is exactly what we mean by the incarnation: they are distinct from one another but they are not separate realities.

Kathleen Raine expresses beautifully the absolute unity of all things.

> Little children have known always
> . . . That the world we see we are: . . .
> Tree, leaf and flower
> Sun, moon and farthest star.[7]

Raine's perception of the oneness of the seer and the seen reiterates Fayan's point that no separate object of our perception has an independent existence of its own; it can be distinguished from another object but it cannot be separated.

St. Thomas Aquinas, a thirteenth-century doctor of the church, puts the same truth philosophically when he says that there can be no dualism, no two realities, when we speak of God and the world. God wears different faces and speaks with different voices, but there is only one reality behind all the masks. Jesus says it most simply of all: at the final judgment the king will say, "I was hungry and you fed me, thirsty and you gave me drink; I was a stranger and you received me into your homes, naked and you clothed me; I was sick and you took care of me, in prison and you visited me." And the righteous will be astonished and ask, "When did we see you . . . ?" (Matthew 25:31–46). The righteous seemingly were charitable but did not understand that the hungry, the thirsty, and the sick were, in fact, the "king." Yet the parable tells us that when we touch our neighbor, we do not only touch a friend of Christ's, we touch Christ himself. When we touch Christ, we touch the one who sent him.

Perhaps a story that was told to me will give us a modern-day version of the incarnation theme. Some years ago I invited Mitch Snyder to visit Saint Peter's College and to speak to our students about his work for the homeless in Washington, D.C. Mitch told us that one winter day he saw a group of blind, homeless people huddled together in a doorway trying to keep warm. Mitch exclaimed that he looked up to heaven and prayed with anger, "God, look at this. I can tolerate blind people and I can tolerate homeless people, but not people who are both blind and homeless. This is too much. God, what are you going to do about it?" Mitch explained that God answered him on the spot. God said, "Mitch, look at this. I can tolerate blind people and I can tolerate homeless people, but not people who are both blind and homeless. This is too much. Mitch, what are you going to do about it?" Mitch did do something about it. One of the many things he did was to live and sleep on a grate with the homeless from the first to the last day of winter to share something of their needs so as to better respond to them. In a Zenlike attitude we ask ourselves: Who was it who lived and slept with the homeless? Was it God or was it Mitch? Or was it God with Mitch or was it Mitch with God? Or was it Mitch and God? We must be careful here when we say Mitch "and" God. In Zen thought Mitch and God are neither identical nor are they different. They cannot be divided; they are just the way they are. Consequently neither can the compassion they feel toward the homeless be divided. They are both completely Mitch and completely God, and completely the homeless. Whatever Mitch is, God is; Mitch is a complete manifestation of the absolute but he is not the only manifestation. Whatever God is, God is not just Mitch. Just as for Zen the Absolute is never exhausted by the relative so too for us God is not exhausted by any one of his manifestations.

Pondering the verse of the 17th koan we can stretch our mind to see clearly the unity of God and Mitch, of heaven and earth, of the ox and herdsman:

> When a fly sits on the balance, it tilts;
> The balance scale of myriad ages shows up unevenness.
> Pounds, ounces, drams, and grains—you see them clearly;
> But after all it finally reverts and gives up my zero point.[8]

The verse challenges us to see with the eyes of a Zen Buddhist who sees things as not identical; that is, they are distinct from one another. But when the balance reverts to zero: that is, when we are talking about reality, all these are one. The absolute is incarnate in the relative. For if they differ by even a "hairsbreadth," they are as distant as heaven is from the earth, and consequently can never be united as one.

To emphasize again the Zen experience of the "not identical, not different" unity of the absolute and the relative: that is, the unity between God and the world, between Buddha and the great earth, between you and me, I have chosen another beautiful poem by Kathleen Raine. "Seen in a Glass" touches on the theme of the unity of the absolute and the relative:

> Behind the tree, behind the house, behind the stars
> Is the presence that I cannot see
> Otherwise than as house and stars and tree.
> Tree, house, and stars
> Extend to infinity within themselves
> Into the mystery of the world
>
> . . .
>
> Upheld by being that I cannot know
> In other form than stars and stones and trees
> Assume in nature's glass, in nature's eyes.[9]

Raine does not say we are upheld by being we do not know, but that we are upheld by being we "cannot know/ in other form than stars and stones and trees." And although Raine's incarnational insight is clear, if we read that the "presence" is separate from the house, stars, and trees, then it does not extend to the Zen perception of oneness. For Zen there is no "being behind" the house and stars. "Being behind" implies something somehow at least a "hairsbreadth" different. If that is the case the presence and the stars, house, and trees are separated by the "distance between heaven and earth." For Zen, if the absolute is not joined to the relative — that is, one with the relative — it is absolutely unknowable. The verse of the 43rd koan of *The Record of Transmitting the Light* sums up this insight quite beautifully:

If you release a black bird at night,
It flies clothed in snow.[10]

The black bird (absolute) even at night is clothed in snow (relative.) The black bird at night is the unknowable absolute. Wherever it flies, it is covered with the snow of the visible relative moment. Incarnation then, the gift Zen offers here, encourages us to appreciate deeply that God is fully incarnate at every moment in the whole of creation.

This sense of the oneness of all forms is dramatized in the 42nd koan of *The Record of Transmitting the Light*. Master T'ung-an asks a monk, "What's beneath the monk's robe you're wearing?" The monk has no answer. Then T'ung-an says, "Studying the Buddha way and living as a monk and still having no insight is a most painful thing. Now, you ask me the same question." The monk asks: "What's beneath the monk's robe you're wearing?" T'ung-an answers, "Intimacy." The monk is greatly awakened.[11] What insight did the monk gain to be enlightened? What does the monk experience that suddenly awakens him? We can truly say he arrived at the realization that intimacy means there is not a hairsbreadth difference between the absolute and himself.

The verse reflects the experience of the monk:

The water is clear to the very bottom;
The pearl gleams naturally,
without need of cutting and polishing.[12]

To receive the insight that awakens and enlightens the monk is similar to our looking to the bottom of the ocean and seeing the pearl in the moment of creation, of incarnation. It is experiencing the presence of the absolute that makes one see the pearl gleam and the pebbles sparkle.

Reading Emily Dickinson's poetry we know she would have been at home with this picture of the ox herdsman because of its incarnational theme and his sheer joy at experiencing his unity with the absolute. In one of her deceptively lighthearted poems she shares with us her deep conviction of the incarnation of the absolute in the relative, not just in Christ but in all creation.

The Brain is just the weight of God —
For — Heft them — Pound for Pound —
And they will differ — if they do —
As Syllable from Sound.[13]

As with our Zen authors "sound and syllable" for Dickinson are not identical but not different either.

In a poem she specifically titles "Incarnation" Kathleen Raine also
celebrates the union portrayed in this ox-herding picture. In this lyric
she dramatizes the unfolding of the speaker's gradual discovery of the
oneness of all things. Beautifully she portrays the speaker's imagination
visualizing the incarnation expanding boundaryless until it includes all
of reality: "not identical but not separate." Joy, for example, is distinct
from sorrow, but not different. No matter the distinction, the absolute is
incarnate in the relative and cannot be separated from it:

At the day's end I found

Nightfall wrapped around a stone.
I took the cold stone in my hand,
The shadowy surfaces of life unwound,
And within I found
A bird's fine bone.

I warmed the relic in my hand
Until a living heart
Beat, and the tides flowed
Above, below, within.

There came a boat riding the storm of blood
And in the boat a child,

In the boat a child
Riding the waves of song,
Riding the waves of pain.[14]

For her part Emily Dickinson reveals the absolute in the image of the sea, which envelops her speaker, the relative. Dickinson's speaker, similar to Raine's speaker, tells us that her experience was a gradual one:

> But no Man moved me—til the Tide
> Went past my simple Shoe—
> And past my Apron—and my Belt
> And past my Bodice—too-
>
> And made as He would eat me up—
> As wholly as a Dew
> Upon a Dandelion's Sleeve—
> And then—I started—too—
> And He—He followed—close behind—
> I felt His Silver Heel
> Upon my Ankle—Then my Shoes
> Would overflow with Pearl—[15]

Both poems dramatize the speaker's experiencing the reality of the incarnation.

The Zen experience of incarnation is a gift to us precisely because it is expressed differently from our own traditional understanding of Christ's incarnation. Perhaps this gift will either reaffirm our traditional expression of incarnation or it will challenge us to recast, refine, and deepen our traditional expression of faith and open our creed to a new dimension of fresh insight. Surely we must recognize—as did Vatican II—that other religions—like Zen Buddhism, for example—also have a role in the divine. We are called to cooperate with them in the wide area in which our common vocation is at work for the development of the world. At least we should remember the words of St. Maximos telling us that dogmas are not so much answers as questions, questions to which "heresies" are in reality, oversimple or overhasty answers.[16] These questions are what we need to explore to further our understanding of the cosmos in the twentieth century.

We cannot expect the Buddhists, given their history and culture, to experience incarnation the way Christians do. And yet the Buddhists have their own figure of human wisdom and compassion in the magnificent Bodhisattva who closely resembles the personality of Jesus and whose life resembled Christ's life. The Bodhisattva, we are told, puts off entering nirvana until even the grass is enlightened. Still, the Buddhists do not worship this Bodhisattva as one having a separate divine nature; this would imply duality. Zen Buddhists hold that the Bodhisattva's nature and theirs are one. They recognize that this self-giving and compassionate figure of the Bodhisattva is not always a Buddhist; they believe Christ to be a Bodhisattva figure who suffered for others and put their well-being before his own.

I would like to conclude this chapter by giving an example of how Christianity and Buddhism met in the figures of Jesus and the Bodhisattva. During the meeting of the Asian Catholic bishops in Thailand in January 2000, the Vatican directed the bishops to evangelize Asia primarily by proclaiming Jesus as the unique savior of the world. But because they felt they should be sensitive to the enduring Buddhist spirituality of Asia and since they were aware that the Buddhists saw Christ and the Bodhisattva as one, the bishops offered an alternative way to evangelize Asia. They claimed that although they did not deny the uniqueness of Christ, they believed they should not present Christ as simply unique. They proposed to portray both Christ and the church in a way that resembled the Bodhisattva: that is, as humble companions and partners of all Asians in their common quest for the truth.[17] The bishops' recommendation in a way clarifies the Zen concept of the absolute and the relative as one. For to the Buddhists Christ and Bodhisattva are one. Does this Zen gift not challenge us to accept and open our minds and hearts to say with St. Paul: "I live, now not I, but Christ lives in me" (Galatians 2:20).

· VII ·

THE OX DISAPPEARS,
THE HERDSMAN REMAINS

The Gift of Emptiness

Emptiness is form; Form is Emptiness

The herdsman has come home on the back of the ox.
Now there is no ox any longer. The herdsman sits
alone, quiet and at leisure . . .
Singing and dancing, the herdsman leads a leisurely
life, not bound to anything anymore.
Between the sky and the earth he has become his own master.[1]

The journey is complete: the ox herdsman has returned to his origin, his true nature. "Now there is no ox any longer": the ox and the herdsman are one. All the anguish he experienced in his separateness has been put to rest. The poet tells us that the herdsman "is alone, quiet, and at leisure." He is "not bound to anything anymore. . . . he has become his own master." Enlightened, he experiences that all forms are empty. He now sings and dances.

I have chosen the Zen gift of seeing into the emptiness of all things for this ox-herding picture. By "emptiness of all things" the Zen Buddhists mean the co-origination of all things: that is, nothing is separate. Seeing into the emptiness of all forms goes beyond the principle that all the things of this world are impermanent. At this stage of his journey the herdsman experiences that not only are all things impermanent, they are empty: that is, there are really no things in the world at all. Legend credits the sixth-century Chinese Patriarch for the most memorable teaching on the emptiness of all things. In his *Platform Sutra* he states that "Fundamentally not one thing exists."[2] It is most remarkable that Zen teachers so long ago and without the aid of modern science saw into the reality of the world. Today we in the Christian West listen to scientists and philosophers reinforce this centuries-old insight of the Zen Buddhists. In 1997 for example, writing to contemporary religious, Sandra Schneiders tells them:

> The universe . . . is not a free-standing, objective, purely material substance, which we have a right and duty to dominate and exploit for our immediate ends, but an infinite, complex process in which everything is related to everything else and nothing is standing still.[3]

She also asks us of the postmodern world to consider the insights we have gained from physics. And we then question ourselves if we can any longer hold on to claims about unchanging natures and nondiscussible moral absolutes.

Emptiness makes us aware that there are no things that are impermanent and therefore subject to change because "fundamentally not one thing exists." There is literally not even a single speck of dust in the whole universe. David Toolan in his article "Nature is a Heraclitean Fire" writes that the universe is the ebb and flow of energy. The "things" of this world he tells us, are not static entities; instead they are processes in motion. Toolan explains that nature is an immensely complicated communication system. He goes on to say that in each instant we see the emptiness or the interconnectedness of nature that allows no one thing to exist or endure. Consequently there is no free-standing universe apart from the viewer who co-creates his own unique world with all he sees, hears, and perceives. This emptiness, as Toolan describes it, can be aptly expressed as intergenerational dependence, husband and wife, parents and children, young and old. There is nothing that exists independently.[4] Quoting philosopher Alfred North Whitehead, Toolan contends, "There is no nature at an instant."[5]

Agreeing with Toolan and Whitehead, Marie Ponsot in "Even" not only writes about the interdependence of Adam and Eve but also about the fact that Adam and Eve exist only now in the present instant. Ponsot writes:

> Adam wakes present
> in the present tense
> to his present Eve
>   *Eve comes to*
> Adam was nothing
> not even lonely till
> Eve came to
>   listening.[6]

Zen koans by definition particularly tease our mind into an awareness of the emptiness of all things. In the 43rd koan in *The Book of Serenity* a monk asks Master Yantou, "When arising and vanishing go on unceasingly, what then?" Yantou shouts and says, "Whose arising and vanishing is it?"[7] In this koan Yantou is teaching us that the fundamental constant principle of the universe is "moving," but the universe is empty of one who moves: that is, the ordinary person and the enlightened master are fundamentally the same| The koan asks if there is a pure spirit that can exist outside the moving of this universe. For Zen, because human beings cannot know this "pure spirit," it does not exist. That is why the master in the 25th koan in *The Record of Transmitting the Light* throws up his hands at such a question and asks, "What kind of thing would an eternal spirit be?"[8] What the author is asking is what experience do we have of an existence outside of arising and vanishing.

To explain in more detail the Zen gift of emptiness let me give you an example of what I actually experienced. As a young man I taught English as a second language at Rokko High School in Kobe, Japan; I also coached the baseball team. Frequently I still dream about the practice field at the high school and in my dreams I see the mountains behind the school, the inland sea stretching out beyond the city below us, the clouds and the movement caused by the blowing wind. Most of all I see my students as they were years ago, young and fast and—in that particular year of my dream—unbeatable. I hear their voices calling me across the field and I hear their shouts of victory when we win the championship game and carry home the flag of victory. All this exists in my dream and when I wake up, they are all gone: mountains and ocean, students, and shouting are all gone, and I lie awake alone in Jersey City. The existence and reality of all this beauty and activity depend upon my staying asleep, for at the crack of dawn I awake and they vanish. According to the Zen perception, the objects of my dream truly exist—but they are not real; they have no independent existence outside my dream.

When referring to existence the Zen experience is that our waking world is not different from our dreaming world. Everything we experience in our daily lives and in our dreams—mountains and rivers, thoughts and feelings, family and friends—all exist. They may charm us or frighten us. Although one existence is not the other, neither our daily life nor our dream world is real because instead of being independent of our point of view, both are created by it. Our dream world depends on our staying asleep for its existence just as our waking world depends on our staying awake for its existence. Both are empty.

Perhaps in the West no Zen Buddhist gift is as misunderstood as is this gift of emptiness. For Zen, as for modern science, emptiness is not a vacuum. Instead emptiness is all forms: men and women, mountains and rivers, moon and stars; all are considered soulless and in constant flux. The 30th koan in *The Book of Serenity* dramatizes the Zen perception of emptiness. It goes as follows: A monk asks Master Dasui, "When the fire . . . rages through and the whole universe is destroyed, is 'this' destroyed or not?" What does the monk mean by "this?" Most likely because this monk is concerned about the immortality of his very self, he hopes that Master Dasui will say that his self will not perish, and he should set his mind at rest. Instead Master Dasui replies, "Destroyed." Dismayed by the answer of Master Dasui and like a drowning man clutching at a straw, the monk repeats his question using other words: "Then it will be gone with the other?" The "other" here means the universe. Then the axe falls: Master Dasui gives the finishing blow, "It will be gone with the other."⁹ "It" will be gone because there is no independent "it" to begin with.

Greatly discouraged but determined to receive a different answer, the poor monk travels across the whole of China to visit a second master and relates to him his conversation with Master Dasui. This second master immediately offers incense and pays homage to Dasui. He tells the monk that Dasui is a great master, that the monk should return to Dasui, confess his error, and learn from Dasui. The bewildered monk crosses China once more to be reconciled to Master Dasui and his teaching of emptiness. Arriving at Master Dasui's monastery he finds that the master has died. Heartbroken now the monk journeys back again to his second master only to find that he too has died. That they died exemplifies what Zen means by emptiness which goes far beyond the concept of the impermanence of all things. That the masters had no independent existence to begin with explains the Zen meaning of emptiness.

In another koan, the Tang monk, Jingzun, writes about this sad monk running back and forth across China and exclaims that "Clearly there is no other truth" than the Zen experience that all things are empty. There is really no one thing; in the world there is only the exchange of energy. Hence Jingzun wonders how:

> One saying—"it all goes along with the fire"
> Sends a monk running over a thousand mountains.[10]

The Zen gift of emptiness urges us then to see first of all the utter nothingness of the world: looking around we see that there is no thing that can take root or endure or return again because all forms are empty. This gift of emptiness implies that our only home is the present moment as it appears before us over and over again.

In a deceptively simple and humorous poem Wislawa Szymborska explains this concept in language and images that are very familiar to us. Her message is that all we have of life is the present moment and once that is past, it is gone forever. Each moment then is all the reality there is and Zen would add that everything in that moment is empty:

> Nothing can ever happen twice.
> In consequence, the sorry fact is
> that we arrive here improvised
> and leave without the chance to practice.
> Even if there is no one dumber,
> if you're the planet's biggest dunce,
> you can't repeat the class in summer:
> this course is only offered once.[11]

Szymborska repeats this theme of "one time only" in her poem "An Effort." Her speaker mournfully declares her sorrow at discovering the impermanence of life. Ironically Szymborska has this speaker respond to the romantic song "My Love Is Like a Red Red Rose" which sings of the perfection, permanence, and stability of love. Even more than denoting impermanence "An Effort" contradicts the perfection and loving relationship that exists in the original song of Robert Burns. In "An Effort" all the speaker is left with is the appalling realization of "one-time-only to the marrow of my bones." Zen would tell us that Szymborska's two poems convince us that the world we know only exists for us. It is empty; it has no existence outside our imagination. It is not independent of our thoughts. The speaker in "an effort" continues:

> Alack and woe, oh song: you're mocking me;
> try as I may, I'll never be your red, red rose.
> A rose is a rose is a rose. And you know it.

> I worked to sprout leaves. I tried to take root.
> I held my breath to speed things up, and waited
> for the petals to enclose me.

> Merciless song, you leave me with my lone,
> nonconvertible, unmetamorphic body:
> I'm one-time-only to the marrow of my bones.[12]

While there can be humor in perceiving the "one-time-only" characteristic of the world, this perception can cause great suffering, because it stems from and expands upon our understanding of impermanence, which is the first noble truth of Buddhism. The suffering that can be caused by impermanence and emptiness is also the theme of Chekhov's *The Cherry Orchard*. Chekhov does not argue philosophies about what change is and where it comes from or whether it is good or bad. He merely presents a theater-poem of the suffering change causes. The action of the play is "to save the cherry orchard." At the end the family of the play departs, the windows are boarded up, the furniture is piled in the corners, and the bags are packed. All the characters on stage as well as the audience see that the family's wish to save the cherry orchard has in fact destroyed it. Their desire to save it was their refusal to consent to unavoidable change. Chekhov has no other plot or point to his play. He presents the characters' perception of the cherry orchard as the time for decision comes and goes.[13] And what finally is the "cherry orchard"?

If we look at it in the light of the verse in the 8th koan of *The Gateless Gate* we see that the cherry orchard, like all forms, is empty:

Since the cottage has been built by assembling brushwood,
There is nothing but the field,
Even without taking it to pieces.[14]

Another koan reveals the complete interdependence of all "things,"
including ourselves who are by nature integrated with the world. The
27th koan of *The Blue Cliff Records* shows us how positive this experience of emptiness is. In it the great Master Unmon answers a question
from a monk worried about life after death. The monk asks Unmon,
"What will it be when trees wither and leaves fall?" This simple question cannot hide the pain the monk feels as he faces the inevitable end
of his life. Instead of lying to him to alleviate the monk's fear of dying,
Unmon tells him "to become the golden breeze of autumn" and

The wind [that] blows across the plain,
    [and]
[the] soft rain [that] clouds the sky.[15]

Very similar to the conversation or lesson that transpired between
Unmon and the monk are the words of the British Victorian poet Gerard
Manley Hopkins in "Spring and Fall." He tells the child who is crying
over the fallen leaves, that "it is Margaret you mourn for."[16] Yes, in the
fallen leaves she sees herself. Were she able to see into the emptiness of
all things as do the Zen Buddhists, she would know that all things are empty.

The 43rd koan of *The Blue Cliff Records* explains more deeply the
Zen perception of emptiness. It tells the story of a zealous monk who
takes a similar journey to that of the ox herdsman's; in a moment of insight
the monk experiences that all forms are empty because no thing is independent of his perception. He enters the emerald palace that shines in
the moonlight—the condition where seer and seen are one—and finds
the palace empty. He finally recognizes and fully experiences that there
is actually no "world" that is empty of substance; there is only "emptiness shining in the bright moonlight."[17]

Another poetic expression for "emptiness shining in the bright moonlight" is dramatized in the 38th koan of *The Gateless Gate* in which the

author recounts the story about a great ox passing through a window.[18] He explains that the ox's head, horns, and four legs pass through the window but the tail does not. Then the author tests us, "Why do you think his tail can't pass through too?" With this question the author is attempting to stretch our minds to recognize that just as in the ox-herding pictures, this ox stands for our real, ultimate truth — our Buddha nature. The window is an opening into emptiness and although the head, horns, and body of the ox pass through the window, the tail remains to make us realize that even though all things are empty, the world itself still exists. If the tail, the fact of our existence, passes through the window, there would indeed be only a vacuum. Instead of a vacuum we have one another and the world we live in. We and the world are the tail, the "emerald palace shining in the bright moonlight."

The verse of this koan says:

> If it [the tail] passes through [the window], it will fall into a ditch [a vacuum],
>
> . . . .
>
> This tiny little tail,
> What a strange and marvelous thing it is![19]

So the tail remains, wondrous being that it is, beyond thought or explanation teasing us to experience that all is emptiness and that emptiness is not a vacuum.

How can the Zen "view" of emptiness — the presence of co-arising "beings" whose selfhood has been hollowed out — ever be a gift for Christians who have been taught to believe in an immutable divine essence? It can, because, first of all, emptiness is not a view, it is the deconstructor of all views.[20] In fact the great Buddhist philosopher Nagarjuna taught that those who held emptiness as a view should be given up as incurable. Nagarjuna did not cling to theories of essences and he did not cling to theories of emptiness. Practically speaking emptiness can be considered a strategy for negating confrontational patterns of knowing.[21] And this surely is a great gift for anyone, Christian or not, who sits down in meditation and in interfaith dialogue. From so many faiths we come together to sit and meditate in the *zendo*, not to solve a philosophical problem but to experience the emptiness of all our ideas about God and no God, self and no self. Together we enter into the presence of mystery and mutual service. (However, by no means am I saying this is the only way to practice interfaith dialogue. Indeed some interfaith dialogue takes place precisely to confront philosophical problems.)

I believe, reflecting on Mary Oliver's poem "Orion" will help us to understand the Zen experience of emptiness: that no one thing exists independent of the observer:

> I love Orion, his fiery body, his ten stars,
> his flaring points of reference, his shining dogs.
> "It is winter," he says. . . .
>   . . .
>
>   Miles below
> in the cold woods, with the mouse and the owl,
> with the clearness of water sheeted and hidden,
> with the reason for the wind forever a secret,
> he descends and sits with me, his voice
> like the snapping of bones.
>   Behind him
> everything is so black and unclassical; behind him
> I don't know anything, not even
> my own mind.[22]

The Zen gift of insight into emptiness by no means denies the existence of the world. It is rather a healthy reminder that what we see around us is either what we see from our own perspective or what we imagine. In her poem "Robert Shumann" Mary Oliver reflects on the power of our thought processes and imagination. And for me she clarifies the perspective of emptiness:

> Hardly a day passes I don't think of him
> in the asylum: younger . . .

. . . And now I understand
Something so frightening, and wonderful—

how the mind clings to the road it knows, rushing
through crossroads, sticking

like lint to the familiar. So!
hardly a day passes I don't

think of him: nineteen, say, and it is
spring in Germany

and he has just met a girl named Clara.
He turns a corner,

he scrapes the dirt from his soles,
he runs up the dark staircase, humming.[23]

A similar reflection comes from the pen of the humorist H. L. Mencken. He writes that a romantic is one "whose eye inevitably exaggerates, whose ear inevitably hears more than the band plays, whose imagination inevitably doubles and triples the news brought in by his five senses."[24] On this concluding note I hope that in this chapter the koans and poetry referred to have clarified for you the Zen gift of emptiness, which highly recommends that we hear the music being played "now" and that we dance to it "now" for it is "one-time-only" and empty.

· VIII ·

THE COMPLETE DISAPPEARANCE
OF OX AND HERDSMAN
AS SEPARATE

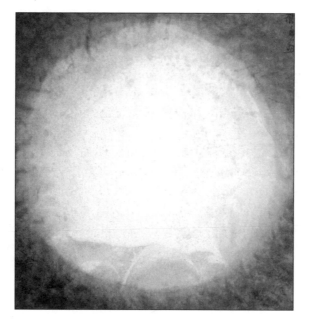

*The Gift of Understanding
That There Is No Separate
Dwelling Place for God* in all

Do not linger where the Buddha dwells
Go quickly past the place where no Buddha dwells.
What is inmost in him can no longer be seen into,
not even by him who has a thousand eyes.[1]

The poet's mandate "not [to] linger where the Buddha dwells" is one more reminder that the Absolute/God/Buddha is not external to the self: the Absolute and the relative are one. On the other hand, the charge, "Go quickly past the place where no Buddha dwells" warns both the herdsman and us not to fall into nihilism. There is an Absolute but since the Absolute is one with the herdsman it "can no longer be seen into/not even by him who has a thousand eyes." The Absolute, be it God or Buddha, exists and is not separate from us.

A similar exhortation awakened the 9th Indian Patriarch, Buddhamitra. He tells us that as a young student he heard his teacher warn:

If you search externally for a Buddha
He will not resemble you.[2]

Hearing this and realizing he should not look outside himself for the Buddha, Buddhamitra writes a verse showing that to be one with the Buddha is to be intimate with the Buddha:

Father and mother are not close to me;
With whom am I most intimate?
The Buddhas are not my way;
With what way am I most intimate?[3]

This verse deals then with the mystery of intimacy and it tells us that to know what intimacy really is, we cannot compare it with the felt intimacy we have with our father and mother whom we see as external to us. Because there is a physical distinction between our parents and ourselves, the intimacy we have with them forms relationships. The intimacy in this verse does not imply relationship; it implies oneness: there is no dialogue because we are one with the absolute. And just as to see and hear we must use our own eyes and ears, so too we must find our own way and not follow the way of a Buddha, which is outside ourselves because that way can never be our way. *outside of us*

Defining intimacy in the Zen Buddhist tradition the 22nd Indian Patriarch, Manorhita, tells us that "not a speck comes from the outside: there is not the slightest separation [between seeing and what is seen]." It's all one. Hence if we define "intimacy" as a relationship with another, then we cannot be "intimate" with a Buddha outside ourselves, because there is no such Buddha. The same goes for our way. Ours is the only way for us; the Buddha's way (if we see the Buddha external to us) is not our way because there is no such way. The verse of this koan says,

> The spirit of [emptiness] is neither inside nor outside;
> Seeing, hearing, forms [of Buddha] are all empty.[4]

For Zen Buddhists there is no such thing as the supernatural outside us. The Buddha, the herdsman, you, and I are one and that one is empty.

The 24th Indian Patriarch, Aryasimha, sheds significant light on the Zen perception that there is no Buddha outside the self. Assertively he tells his monks, "If you have not done this [experienced that there is no Buddha outside of you], then even if you make it rain flowers from the sky and make the earth tremble . . . and discuss the profound and subtle, as far as the true wonderful Way is concerned, you have not glimpsed so much as a hair of it."[5] *they are external signs*

The 41st Master, T'ung-an, even more strongly contends that there is no Buddha outside the self. He says that people who "love" the Buddha as if it were outside themselves add iron shackles to iron shackles: they are born and they die without freedom. T'ung-an would have us banish this love for an external Buddha saying there is nothing we can learn from a Buddha separate from us because no such Buddha exists. Recall the verse that depicts things as they are in themselves and not looking outside themselves for meaning.

> The water is clear to the very bottom;
> The pearl gleams naturally, without need of cutting and polishing.[6]

That is, they just are. They and their function are one and the absolute does not dwell "apart" from them.

In her poem "Psalm" Wislawa Szymborska deplores the human need to be "foreign"—that is, to separate things while the remainder of the world rests in its function and is content in what it is: "the rest is mixed vegetation, subversive moles and wind." She criticizes the human need to create "leaky boundaries of man-made states":

> Oh, the leaky boundaries of man-made states!
> How many clouds float past them with impunity;
> how much desert sand shifts from one land to another;
> how many mountain pebbles tumble onto foreign soil
> in provocative hops!

> Need I mention every single bird that flies in the face of frontiers
> or alights on the roadblock at the border?
> . . .

> Only what is human can truly be foreign.
> The rest is mixed vegetation, subversive moles, and wind.[7]

Just as humans create "leaky boundaries," they also seek help outside themselves. All this speaks of the human sense of incompleteness. In her poem "A Paleolithic Fertility Fetish" Szymborska uses the metaphor of the Great Mother to represent the absolute. She does so to teach us that we should live as we are, "without need of cutting and polishing," without creating "man-made separations" and without external gods. The Great Mother "has no face" because she is no face and all faces; she has no feet and yet she is all feet. There is no separate dwelling place for the Great Mother/ absolute/ God:

The Great Mother has no face.
Why would the Great Mother need a face . . . . .

The Great Mother has no feet.
What would the Great Mother do with feet.
Where is she going to go.
Why would she go into the world's details.
She has gone as far as she wants
and keeps watch in the workshops under her taut skin.[8]

The Great Mother is the absolute. She is focused, attentive, and free of limiting desires. To use Symborska's expression, she is without "the world's details," without the human need "to separate and create boundaries." The Great Mother dwells everywhere and nowhere. She is "neither inside nor outside." She is the absolute.

In yet another poem Symborska writes of the absolute unity of the natural world in just being what it is and in doing what it does in total abandonment to its function. The lake exists in its function; so does the sky. What better manifestation of the nature of the absolute? The poem seems to celebrate the achievement of total being. For humans to achieve this state of acceptance and concentration they have to live life self-contained, second by second in absolute serenity. They must simply function (be) and not be concerned about being; they must experience at every moment that the absolute dwells within them:

The window has a wonderful view of a lake,
but the view doesn't view itself.
It exists in this world
colorless, shapeless,
soundless, odorless, and painless.

The lake's floor exists floorlessly,
and its shore exists shorelessly.
Its water feels itself neither wet nor dry
and its waves to themselves are neither singular nor plural.

They splash deaf to their own noise
on pebbles neither large nor small.

And all this beneath a sky by nature skyless
in which the sun sets without setting at all
and hides without hiding behind an unminding cloud. . . .[9]

Zen Masters teach that there is no Buddha (or absolute) external to us and that the Buddha (our true nature) participates in the whole of reality without boundaries. To live thus is for us to participate in the absolute to the extent that we are capable. Because the masters insist that their teaching is not nihilistic, they constantly remind us of the Absolute within. Indeed koan after koan in *The Record of Transmitting the Light* Zen patriarchs and masters reiterate that different from "some non-Buddhists" they are not nihilists.[10] For Sosan, the 30th Master, to be a nihilist is to live like wood or stone, thus he warns his students against becoming nihilists. And Tao-pi, the 40th Master, argues that the nihilistic view, which contends that not a single thing exists, is not the Zen Buddhist view.[11]

Impressing us with the truth that the Buddha and we exist and are one, the 45th Master, Tao-Kai, speaks of the Buddha, as the "old fellow" (Buddha, the true self) with whom we have lived from the beginning, but whose face is unknown. In another metaphor he writes of life as a road on which no one comes or goes, and yet there is "something (Buddha, the Absolute) that is not emptied out."[12] Also, the 46th Master, Tan-Lsia, repeats the phrase of his master Tao-Kai and teaches that although all things are utterly empty, still there is "something that cannot be emptied." And this "something that cannot be emptied" cannot be seen by looking within or without. The verse following his statement sums up the mystery and seems to tell us to experience that the Buddha and we are one, and not to try to rationalize it:

The icy spring of the valley stream—no one peeks into it.
It does not allow travelers to penetrate its depth.[13]

Although centuries of Zen teachers insist they are not nihilists, they still hold that we can't know any truth or Buddha "outside" the passing forms that make up our early lives. Beyond these forms we can't know, we can't peek into "the icy spring" to see the truth, and we cannot relate to it apart from the forms and functions of our lives. An anonymous Zen poet sums up the Zen patriarchs' teachings saying that it is forbidden to search for the absolute apart from the self:

> Today's ability to avoid what is forbidden
> Surpasses yesterday's most eloquent discussion!

Actually it is forbidden to search for the absolute apart from the self because it is impossible. There is no path to the Buddha, to the truth of our lives but through the dust of our everyday existence. To avoid pondering the imponderable is a great feat: it "surpasses . . . . [the] most eloquent discussion." Not to get involved in such an exercise of futility (searching for the absolute outside the self) calls for tremendous discipline and attention to the present moment. This fundamental teaching of Zen Buddhism—that it is impossible to find the absolute apart or separate from the self (us)—is not a statement of atheism; nor is it a statement even suggesting that the absolute is impersonal. Zen teaches that the absolute simply is unknowable and cannot be known or described through reason. For this reason Zen categorically rejects the various essentialist philosophies that are based on reason and that flourish in both Buddhist and non-Buddhist cultures. Zen insists that it is not through reason but through personal enlightenment that we know what is true. For Zen Buddhists all philosophical thought is mere speculation; even their own view of emptiness is never to be made into an absolute itself. For them, emptiness is simply a descriptive term for the mind of wisdom that sees the illusory status of all verbal statements.

Zen is not disparaging human reason or philosophical thinking. It is simply saying that reason is not the tool for the work of enlightenment. In her poem "Contraband" perhaps Denise Levertov, who contends that it was the human desire to come to knowledge through reason that drove humanity out of Eden and separated it from God, might shed light on the Zen reaction to substituting reason for experience in something so essential as enlightenment:

The tree of knowledge was the tree of reason.
That's why the taste of it
drove us from Eden. That fruit
was meant to be dried and milled to a fine powder
for use a pinch at a time, a condiment.
God had probably planned to tell us later
about this new pleasure.

In the line "God had probably planned to tell us later," Levertov seems to suggest that through attentiveness, not weakened by indulgence, we would have arrived at "this new pleasure." But instead of integrating reason with all the other gifts we received in Eden: insight, memory, sensation, and language, she sadly tells us, we allow reason to overcome us and so separate us from God/Paradise:

We stuffed our mouths full of it,
gorged on *but* and *if* and *how* and again
but, knowing no better.
It's toxic in large quantities; fumes
swirled in our heads, and around us
to form a dense cloud that hardened to steel,
a wall between us and God, who was Paradise.

By no means is Levertov suggesting that reason is not a "good." What she is telling us is that reason, like any other good used to excess, dehumanizes us. Hers is a wake-up call to attentiveness. It's the same call we have been hearing throughout the entire journey of the ox herdsman. Reason used to excess (like any other good) "lock[s] us into our own limits"—it separates us so that we cannot participate in the world of reality without boundaries:

Not that God is unreasonable—but reason
in such excess was tyranny
and locked us into our own limits, a polished cell
reflecting our own faces.

Levertov concludes that reason, when excessive, is tyrannous. As such it is always inadequate to the task of capturing truth and expressing it in unambiguous language. Actually all excess reflects "our own faces," which reveal "our own limits." She contends that clinging to reasoned truths and imagined realities is the cause of delusion and primal ignorance, which according to John Keenan can become the source of metaphysical arrogance and delusional religious certitude. Interestingly Levertov portrays God as lovingly piercing through the slits of "reasoned" barriers.

> . . . God lives
> on the other side of that mirror,
> but through the slit where the barrier doesn't
> quite touch ground, manages still
> to squeeze in—as filtered light,
> splinters of fire, a strain of music heard
> then lost, then heard again.[14]

However, if we grasp at the light, the fire, and the music, and if we stubbornly hold on to them, to possess them (as if there were anything outside ourselves that could be possessed), we will block up "the slit where the barrier doesn't quite touch the ground," and prevent God from "squeezing in." *we will only see or know that but*

In her poem "First Snow" Mary Oliver unfolds a beautiful natural scene reminding us of how often we try to "obstruct" the beautiful with our need to know "why." Still nature remains and is what it is. the energy never ebbs, the snow never settles less than lovely, the silence is immense, the heavens still hold a million candles and for all our questions there are no answers. If we could but focus on the total harmony and unity of the universe, we would not question everything. We would not need to possess; we would not build barriers to separate what was never separate:

> The snow
> began here
> this morning and all day
> continued, its white

rhetoric everywhere
calling us back to *why, how,*
whence such beauty and *what*
the meaning; such
an oracular fever! flowing
past windows, an energy it seemed
would never ebb, never settle
less than lovely! and only now,
deep into night,
it has finally ended.
The silence
is immense,
and the heavens still hold
a million candles;

. . .

and though the questions
that have assailed us all day
remain—not a single
answer has been found—[15]

[handwritten marginal note: The more ans we think we have the more questions]

Because we "search" for fullness outside ourselves, we hunger for, cling to, the security of an answer in the form of a theory or an idea. This, because we search outside of ourselves for truth! Oliver writes of this human obsession in the first half of her poem "Sunrise" and in the concluding half she invites us to experience a moment which for her was one of true enlightenment. Totally abandoned to the moment of beauty, she becomes all and nameless. To have a name, to be separate, is not to be alive to the beauty of the moment.

> You can
> die for it—
> an idea,
> or the world. People
>
> have done so,
> brilliantly,

letting
their small bodies be bound

to the stake,
creating
an unforgettable
fury of light. But

this morning,
climbing the familiar hills
in the familiar
fabric of dawn, I thought
. . .
how the sun

blazes
for everyone just
so joyfully
as it rises

under the lashes
of my own eyes, and I thought
I am so many!

What is my name?[16]

Oliver's question, "what is my name?" recalls the question of the verse accompanying this ox-herding picture: "what is my way?" To know one's name is to know that one is one with the absolute and to experience this is to know one's "way" reinforcing the message. The last koan of *The Gateless Gate* tells us of a monk who in all earnestness questions Master Kempo, "In the ten directions, there is one way to the gate of nirvana. I wonder where the way is." In response Kempo lifts up his staff, draws a line in the sand, and says, "Here it is."[17] Because the monk does not understand, he asks again and again, and every time he does Master

Kempo lifts up his staff and draws a line in the sand and says, "Here it is." Finally the monk understands the gesture of his master. He perceives that even though there are ten directions, every direction is the one straight way to nirvana; the way is not only where Master Kempo draws a line; it is everywhere and every time we stand or sit or speak. No matter how long and how often we search outside ourselves we will find no Buddha; no matter in which direction we look for the way outside ourselves, we will never find a direction that can be called our way. We are the Buddha (God dwells in us) and the roadless road within ourselves is the way. If we know who we are, everyplace and every direction is our way.

Can we Christians not hear in this Zen gift Christ's words: "I am the way, the truth, and the life" (John 14:6)? Can this Zen gift of no God outside ourselves help us to really understand that we are Christ himself? St. Augustine tells us that in the end there will be only one Christ loving himself. And when he was bishop of Hippo, St. Augustine would hold up the Eucharist at liturgies and exhort his Christian followers to come and "receive what you are"; not what you could be or will be, but what you are.

· IX ·

THE RETURN TO THE ORIGIN

The Gift of No-Self—
Transformation into the Absolute

Returned to the ground and origin, the herdsman
Has completed everything.
Nothing is better than . . . to be as blind
and deaf.
Boundlessly flows the river, just as it flows. Red
blooms the flower, just as it blooms[1]

Having returned to "the ground and origin," his true nature, the herds-man has completed his journey. He is now ready to give up the attach-ments and limitations associated with the separate individual self; the searcher has become one with the universe. "Nothing is better than . . . to be as blind / and deaf" because now he does not have limited sight and hearing. Being totally one with the universe is to hear and see all, to live totally in the present moment. Hence the "transformation" of the individual self into the whole. The individual consciousness breaks through its limitations and arrives at the wonderful sense of fullness and wholeness. Because of the ox herdsman's transformation the poet tells us that for him finally, "Boundlessly flows the river just as it flows. Red blooms the flower, just as it blooms." Everything is as it is—selfless and unpreoccupied with selfish limitations.

The koan I have chosen to help us reflect on the extraordinary gift this ox-herding picture presents is one that depicts the enlightenment and the transformation of the 4th Patriarch, Upagupta. The author tells us that one day while Upagupta is attending his master, Sanavasa, the mas-ter questions him, "Did you make your home departure physically or in spirit?" To which Upagupta replies, "Truly, I made my home departure physically." His master questions him, "How can the wondrous dharma of the Buddhas have anything to do with body or mind?" On hearing this, Upagupta is awakened. He grasps the meaning that because there is no self separate from the whole, there is no distinction or detail such as a "body or mind" related to an empty form.[2]

When Upagupta realizes there is no-self to depart from home then, as the koan instructs, he never again hankers after anything such as his true nature, the holy truth, the elimination of his passions, or the attainment of enlightenment. For he now knows that everything is empty. And although, the koan tells us, he understands that "he is and he is not," he also knows that he has no existence separate from the whole. The author goes on to tell us that when Upagupta hears "how can the dharma of the Buddhas have anything to do with body and mind?" the words resound "like a clap of thunder." He feels as if "the roots of his ears [are] cut off." Indeed he actually becomes deaf. The verse of the koan reflects the awakening of Upagupta:

> House demolished, the person perished, neither inside nor outside,
> Where can body and mind hide their forms?[3]

This verse depicts the wonderful transformation of Upagupta from a limited "is and is not" self into the whole. And transformation into the absolute or the whole as an enlightened way to live is not only a Buddhist way of thinking; other world religions encourage it, especially Christianity. We know St. Paul's words, "I live, now not I, but Christ lives in me"(Galatians 2:20). For Christians transformation into Christ entails becoming what Zen Buddhists call a no-self and although this gift may be painful for us to contemplate and accept, we know that to find our life in Christ we must die to self. Assuredly many poets have written about losing everything and the risk involved for neglecting to do so. In his poem, "NO ONE KNOWS WHETHER DEATH, WHICH MEN IN THEIR FEAR CALL THE GREATEST EVIL, MAY NOT BE THE GREATEST GOOD," after he shows us how in the world of nature it is expedient to die, Daniel Berrigan takes us to scriptures to recall and meditate on the words of Christ. He tells us "unless the grain falling to earth die, itself remains alone":

> It may be expedient to lose everything.
> The moon says it, waxing in silence, the fruit of the heavens,
> grape vine, melon vine.
> Autumn upon us, the exemplar, the time of falling.

One who has lost all is ready to be born into all:
buddha moon   socratic moon   jesus moon
light and planet and fruit of all:
"unless the grain falling to earth die, itself remains alone."[4]

And the poet, Kabir, writes a poem in which line by line he depicts the canceling of details until nothing is left. Reflecting on his poem we understand more clearly the words of the preceding koan, "house demolished," and we can actually experience our own gradual transformation or at least recognize that we too must empty ourselves of the "wanting creature inside" us:

I said to the wanting-creature inside me:
What is this river you want to cross?
There are no travelers on the river-road, and no road.
Do you see anyone moving about on that bank, or resting?
There is no river at all, and no boat, and no boatman.
There is no towrope either, and no one to pull it.
There is no ground, no sky, no time, no bank, no lord!
And there is no body, and no mind![5]

The speaker of the poem holds a dialogue with himself. He does not call his "wanting part" "self" but simply "creature." The speaker seems to come to enlightenment before our eyes. He sees emptiness itself and not even empty forms. He experiences sheer exaltation at the realization that "there is no body and no mind." While the entire poem details the verse of the koan, the final line really echoes the words of Master Sanavasa to Upagupta: "How can the wondrous dharma of the Buddhas have anything to do with body and mind," and reminds us of Upagupta's transformation.

In a Zen-influenced Japanese haiku of the nineteenth century we are given another glimpse at transformation: the road of life with no separate selves on it. We admire the fullness of life happening at the moment of reading the poem. "Autumn Darkness Falls" contains the whole of life. All is transformed into the beauty of the autumn darkness:

Kono michi wa
Yuku hito nashi ni
Aki no Kure.

This road
with no one walking on it
Autumn darkness falls.

That "no one [is] walking on [the road]" reflects the Zen Buddhists'
teaching of no-self while it reinforces their emphasis on the emptiness
or the interdependence of all things. Of course Zen admits that the physical self as well as other physical selves are separate forms in the same
sense that our left hand is not our right hand, and you are not I and I am
not you. But for Zen Buddhists the self in which "we live and have our
being" is utterly one with the passing phenomena that float before our
eyes: "Autumn darkness falls."

For us Westerners to understand the Zen teaching concerning no separate self and to embrace the absolute and not cling to any one form, it
might help us to compare accepting this Zen teaching to learning the
Chinese art of calligraphy the way Simon Lays explains it in his review
of Jean Francois Billeter's *The Chinese Art of Writing*:

> When two great civilizations, utterly foreign to each other, come
> into direct contact, it seems that, at first, they cannot exchange
> anything but blows and trinkets. Mutual access to the core of their
> respective cultures necessitates a lengthy and complex process. It
> demands patience and humility, for outsiders are normally not
> allowed beyond a certain point: they will not be admitted to the
> inner chambers of the spirit, unless they are willing to shed some
> of their original baggage. Cultural initiation entails metamorphosis
> [transformation] and we cannot learn any foreign values if we do
> not accept the risk of being transformed by what we learn.[6]

According to Lays then to practice calligraphy we must learn first about
the brush, the ink, and the paper. We must develop a degree of sensitiv-

ity and a tremendous capacity to see and listen. Once we have done this quite competently, we are in a position to achieve something quite similar to the achievement of those, who in the spiritual life, achieve complete forgetfulness of self: we are ready to be transformed. When Simon Lays says that forgetfulness of self or transformation of self is necessary to accomplish an art form like calligraphy, then transformation of self is even more essential for us if we are to practice *zazen* and accept the gifts Zen has to offer and be awakened to realize our oneness of being with God/ Absolute.

Literature has many examples of characters who through attentiveness and enlightenment are transformed utterly. Iris Murdoch more than once in her novels focuses on the theme of transformation. In *The Good Apprentice* Murdoch uses the myth of Apollo and Marsyas to illustrate the superhuman effort demanded of us for transformation to happen. Myths are stories that we create to explain the unexplainable; the myth of Apollo and Marsysas falls into the death/life genre, which shows us how we must die to self to be transformed into the whole. For the purposes of this novel Murdoch dwells on the scene in which Apollo tortuously flays Marsyas who, though in terrible pain, lovingly gazes on Apollo because he longs for transformation. Once having established the myth, Murdoch uses it to show us how to transcend our human limitations.

One of her characters, Thomas, a psychiatrist and very much an Apollo figure, flays not the skin but the illusions of his patients. No longer believing in dreaming along with his patients and playing the doctor in an endless therapeutic drama of mutual need, he views his new role in life as a servant calling his patients from the sterile, illusory lives they are leading. As such Thomas tries to communicate to them the spiritual force they need to choose the death that leads to life. That is death to illusions and transformation into a life of wholeness and reality. Taking upon himself his special task, as he now understands it, the psychiatrist shows his patients their need to die to themselves in order to live fully. He purports to bring life, "transformation" to the awareness of people who would never on their own have been able to do it for themselves.[7]

Transformation of character is the focus of much of Murdoch's writing. That she may have been influenced by the Zen method is possible.

Sefton, one of Murdoch's characters in *The Green Knight* actually says she thinks that Buddhism is "quite the best" of world religions.[8] Zen Buddhism has always mandated the practice of emptying the self, especially of its ego, and has always declared the ego a limiting human characteristic because of its capacity to alter perception and behavior. Similarly in their writings, Murdoch and Simone Weil consider the destruction of the ego morally essential and certainly a prerequisite to transformation.

Both Murdoch and Weil are very close to the Zen spirit in their writings when they acclaim that the ego or the limited self is obsessive. Both writers believed that it is obsessive, repetitive behavior that obscures our vision of the whole, of the present moment and leads us to be tunnel visioned and opened to perform every kind of selfish deed. And selfishness, we all know, triggers our need to control others and even coerce them into feeding our selfish desires and fears. What even becomes more debilitating for the selfish ego is its need for approval from the people it wishes to control.

In Murdoch's *A Fairly Honorable Defeat*, Julius, a quasi-satanic figure, speaking about selfish and undisciplined people, says that they force others to play any role that feeds their present needs. Julius also characterizes these selfish people as people who are incapable of knowing reality. They either imitate others, reject them, or control them. Perhaps voicing Murdoch's views of failed human beings, Julius tells Morgan:

> Human beings are roughly constructed entities full of indeterminacies and vaguenesses and empty spaces. Driven along by their own private needs they latch blindly onto each other, then pull away, then clutch again. Their little sadisms and masochisms are surface phenomena. Anyone will do to play the roles. They never really see each other at all. There is no relationship, dear Morgan, which cannot quite easily be broken and there is none the breaking of which is a matter of any genuine seriousness. Human beings are essentially finders of substitutes.[9]

For Murdoch, Weil, and Zen Buddhists, to mature into whole human beings demands self-discipline and attention. And to see through our self-made myths in order to rid ourselves of the reactive emotional patterns we were roped into early in life requires struggle and total concentration. To be successful in this endeavor we need to start out on a spiritual journey similar to the ox herdsman's and with the same readiness to empty ourselves of all that stands in the way of our transformation. We know that not all who promise themselves to arrive at their journey's end are successful, and true to life Murdoch shows us that not all of her characters grow up. She shows us people who refuse to change, and in so doing she describes the terrible results of a failure at transformation. It seems Murdoch created these characters to warn her readers against such a tragedy.

In *The Sea, the Sea,* for example, Murdoch demonstrates how the fixation on an adolescent romance inhibits an adult, Charles, from facing reality.[10] Quite the opposite he pursues a woman created by his own obsessions, perceptions, and projections. It seems Murdoch, very much in the spirit of Thomas Merton, would have us examine our own projections in the light of our fears and selfish needs. In *The Good Apprentice* Murdoch goes a step further. One of her characters, Stuart, comes to realize that the obsessions we put into motion at an early age stamp their limitations on us. Because he himself uses every excuse not to be transformed, he blames his failure for not living in reality on life as he perceives it: sex, drink, ambition, pride, cupidity, and soft living.[11] Over and over again in her novels Murdoch describes the barriers people set up to hide behind in order to resist transformation.

Just as we see many agents of transformation in literature, so too we see them in real life. For his part Richard Rohr, a Franciscan priest, contends that priests are agents of transformation. But priests, he says, need not be ordained priests, nor need they be men at all. Instead Rohr recognizes as priests all men and women who assist others in the process of being transformed into new life. He associates this healing transformation with three symbols: the knife, fire, and blood—the knife that cuts off illusions; the fire that transforms all it touches; the blood that heals the afflictions of body and mind. Rohr contends that unless we are able to search for and submit to a life-saving death of the self, we may end up like the old pastor in the play and movie *Mass Appeal* who at the end of his life tells his spiritually searching young curate: "I never knew Christ. I tap danced right past him."[12]

Much more than "priests," the Eucharist is *par excellence* the agent of transformation. Interestingly, Father Aloysius Pieris, S.J., founder of the Tulane Research Center in Sri Lanka, introduced an Asian celebration of the Eucharist founded on his experience of the Zen Buddhist practice of attentiveness and selflessness. Father Pieris teaches and prepares Christians for this "transformational" liturgy at the East Asian Pastoral Institute in Manila. For those Christians in the West who feel called to sit at the Lord's table for contemplatives, this "transformational" liturgy would be a spiritually rewarding experience. In *America* Monsignor Gerald Martin's statement reminds us of Father Pieris's insight into and writings about a "transformational" liturgy: He writes

> Jesus did not institute the Eucharist to change bread and wine into his body and blood, but to change us into his body. The Mass is not meant to transform elements, but to transform people. When he said, "Behold I am with you always, until the end of the world," Jesus was not referring to his real presence in the Eucharist; he was referring to his real presence in his people, the members of his body.[13]

Even if this teaching is commonly accepted in the church today, it is not always commonly put into practice. Believing this to be the sad truth, Father Pieris quotes Vladimir Rozanov's comments, which would agree with Pieris's opinions: "In the West they actually don't worship. Instead, they have a lecture followed by a concert."[14] Pieris writes that verbosity has marred the postconciliar renewal of Catholic liturgy with the intrusion of "shared prayer," which frequently is neither shared nor prayer but instead a composing and recitation of speeches to God and to one another. This opinion may well seem harsh to the many Christians who experience transformation into Christ in the liturgy just as it is. These Christians often resent priests who introduce change to suit their own personal piety.

However to those Christians in the East and West who come together for silent contemplative prayer, Father Pieris's instructions underline the importance of the Zen gifts we have been reviewing: attentiveness to practice, not knowing, transformation.

The Eucharist then is meant to transform us into Christ, to help us to be one with Christ. The Zen experience of no-self can remind us that there is no transformation from one thing into another thing. Transformation in the Eucharist means that we are brought to see the one reality that is present always. As Bodhidharma, the founder of Chinese Zen, said in the sixth century A.D., your true nature is always right "in front of you"—you yourself just do not see it.[15]

How can Zen assist Christians to understand this one reality that is always present "in front of us"? Speaking to us in our theological language, Zen Buddhists would say that Christ and the Father are one, and to say that there are two persons is misleading. There is only one God with one intelligence, one will, and one salvific intent. The Father is everything invisible in the Son and the Son is everything visible in the Father. They are one beyond any duality. Analogously there is no duality between God and the world. They are not two things or separate realities. They would agree with St. Thomas Aquinas that creation adds nothing to the sum total of reality and that the world is the manifestation of its creator and adds nothing to the creator's existence. They would say that Jesus is the incarnation of God and the sign or sacrament of what we too are and must always be.

Zen Buddhists would claim that the union of the absolute and the relative in Jesus is not an absolutely unique miracle that excludes the rest of humanity, and that analogously you and I are not two separate realities but one. They would very much contend with St. Augustine that there is only one Christ loving himself, one reality with many faces. And finally since the absolute and relative can never be separated, they would hold that there is no separation between the Jesus of history and the universal Christ of faith, and that the Eucharist is not a sign pointing to a distant God but a fact revealing the eternally present Father, Christ, you, and me. For Zen Buddhists what can be distinguished must never be separated.

The Zen Buddhist would agree completely that the Eucharist is not just a symbol that points to or represents an absent reality. Rather the Eucharist renders present what it expresses. This bread and wine is the body and blood of Christ. So similarly are the mountains and rivers the body and blood of Christ. What else could the universe possibly be?

Mary Oliver in her poem "Blue Heron" asks the same question:

> Like a pin
> of blue lightning
> it thrusts
> among the pads,
>
> plucking up
> frogs, flipping them
> in mid-air, so that they
> slide, neatly
>
> face-first, down
> the long throat.
> I don't know
> about God,
>
> but didn't Jesus say:
> "This is my body,"
> meaning, the bread —
> and meaning, also,
>
> the things of this world?
> This isn't really
> a question.
> It is the hard
>
> and terrible truth
> we live with,
> feeding ourselves
> every day . . .[16]

The mind, Zen insists, is not a thing we possess; it is whatever we see or hear: bread and wine, mountains and rivers. And Zen Buddhists would agree with us that the Eucharist is not a thing but an action involving the mutual presence and interpenetration of Christ and the faithful. Christians may, but need not, hold an essentialist philosophy that sees an essential separation between the divine and the human. They may, but need not, explain the presence of Christ in the Eucharist by tran-substantiation. They may also believe that Christ is present in the

Eucharist through a change in purpose (transfinalization), or through a change in the meaning of signs (transignification), or through a combination of these philosophical explanations. They may say simply that this bread is still bread—there has been no physical change at all—but it is also the body of Christ.[17]

If some Christians can not reconcile a Zen understanding of no-self with the Christian belief in the transformation of self into Christ in the Eucharist, at least let us together ponder and admire the poem "One or Two Things" by Mary Oliver. In it she advises us not to love our "separate" life too much for that cannot endure.

> For years and years I struggled
> just to love my life. And then
>
> the butterfly
> rose, weightless, in the wind.
> "Don't love your life
> too much," it said,
>
> and vanished
> into the world.[18]

The phrase "Don't love your life too much" recalls the words from scripture with which Daniel Berrigan ended his poem: "Unless the grain falling to earth die, itself remains alone."

· X ·

ENTERING THE MARKET
WITH OPEN HANDS

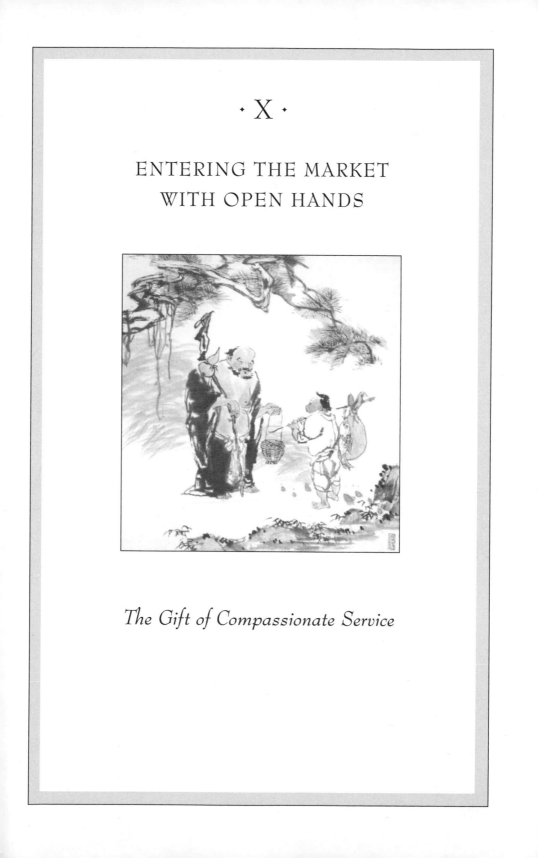

The Gift of Compassionate Service

With bare chest and feet he enters the market.
His face is smeared with earth, his head covered with ashes.
A huge laugh streams over his cheeks.
Without humbling himself to perform miracles or
wonders, he suddenly makes the withered trees bloom.[1]

The half-dozen lines that accompany the tenth and final ox-herding picture bring a happy end to a lifelong and arduous journey. Entering the marketplace the ox herder is a complete human being: that is, he knows he is one with all that is. His "bare chest and feet" signify the epitome of the natural poverty of one who neither clings to possessions, nor adorns himself with trinkets of any kind, nor fills his mind with idle speculation. Indeed he is like an open book to all who see him. His face "smeared with earth, his head covered with ashes" paradoxically contrasts wonderfully with "a huge laugh streams over his cheeks." The contrast reminds us that he has reached "ground and origin," his true nature. Now his is a simple and arduous life; one lived in continuous joy. Describing his joy, the poet uses the word "streams" to reinforce the herdsman's continuous and total insightful living in the present moment. For it is only enlightenment that purifies our compassionate service from self-seeking.

Very importantly the poet tells us that our ox herder is neither a magician nor a worker of wonders. He knows himself; he does not need tricks to offer signs or point to far-off truths. And because he is in touch with life, his very presence is the wondrous miracle that makes "withered trees bloom." Just as the trees, so too all in his presence, opened to the moment, gain insight into being and become enlightened. It is when one arrives at this understanding that one dedicates one's life to the compassionate service of others. And this service is not contrived or deliberate or separate; it flows as the natural function of the truly enlightened person.

To reflect on this final ox-herding picture I have chosen to combine the 50th and 51st koans from *The Record of Transmitting the Light* because together they give us a very clear example of compassionate service in the marketplace.[2] Because intellectual insight into enlightenment certainly does not prepare us for compassionate service, I have decided to share with you my understanding of a conversation that took place eight hundred years ago. Reading it you will see that although many changes have occurred in Zen Buddhism since then, the basic ingredients for enlightenment endure. Enlightenment must be experienced; it is not a theory.

The significant conversation takes place between Dogen and his friend Lao-hsin in China. Dogen is a brilliant young monk who at the age of seven experienced the profound grief of his mother's death. Adopted by the chief advisor to the reigning emperor, Dogen became the sole legitimate heir to Myozen of China. Although today Dogen is considered one of the greatest Zen philosophers and teachers, he was not always imbued with the deepest Zen spirit. Listen to a conversation between Dogen and his friend Lao-hsin which took place two years after Dogen's arrival in China where he had come with Master Myozen to test and hone his skills in dharma combat with the best that Chinese Zen had to offer. This conversation takes place just before Dogen is to return to Japan.

Lao-hsin:	Well, my young friend, so you're going home to Japan!
Dogen:	Yes, it's time. Two years is a long time.
Lao-hsin:	Can I help you with your shopping? Have you bought enough trinkets to take home with you?
Dogen:	Yes, yes, quite enough trinkets.
Lao-hsin:	And do you have enough stories of exotic China to entertain your students and to impress them with your travels?
Dogen:	Oh, yes, quite enough stories and travels.
Lao-hsin:	And those wonderful dharma combats with all the old and pompous abbots and masters. What a joy to see you demolish their pretensions and expose their ignorance! Not one of them dares to debate with you again about Buddhism. You know you don't have an equal in China!

Dogen:	Yes, I've heard that said (Dogen opens his hands in a gesture of acceptance), and it's true; there's no point denying it.
Lao-hsin:	Of course they say you're talkative and arrogant, but that's just because they're jealous of you.
Dogen:	(Laughing) Yes, I know I talk a lot, but why is that not correct?
Lao-hsin:	(After a long pause and changing the topic.) Why do you look a little sad?
Dogen:	(Dogen turns quickly toward his friend as if he has been found out. About to say he isn't sad, he is far too clever to deny the obvious so he confides in Lao-hsin.) Well, my friend, there has to be more to Zen than undressing silly abbots in public.
Lao-hsin:	Indeed there is. (Nodding agreement and encouraged to probe further.) And you've had enough of that?
Dogen:	Quite enough of that, more than enough!
Lao-hsin:	(Looking out the window.) Perhaps then, you're ready . . . for the real thing.
Dogen:	(For the second time Dogen turns sharply to his friend. Has he underestimated this man, a traveling companion, who now seems to be reading his mind?) Of course I'm ready for the real thing, but I have not found it in China.
Lao-hsin:	But you haven't yet met Ju-ching!
Dogen:	Who is Ju-ching?
Lao-hsin:	(Quietly) Ju-ching, Ju-ching is . . . the real thing.
Dogen:	(Turns to his friend and stands speechless before him.) You mean he . . .
Lao-hsin:	Quite so, they say it is very rare . . .
Dogen:	(Raising his voice—which he has never done before in his life.) Why wasn't I told this before?
Lao-hsin:	Oh, Ju-ching doesn't debate young monks looking for a fight. He doesn't even accept invitations to speak with the Emperor!
Dogen:	Who is Ju-ching?
Lao-hsin:	(With the hook now firmly imbedded in Dogen, Lao-hsin tries another tactic.) It's too late now, your ticket is bought,

your souvenirs are wrapped, go home and become an abbot. Why, with your connections at court you'll become a National Teacher!

Dogen: (Begging) Who is Ju-ching?

Lao-hsin: It's a long story . . .

Dogen: (Urging) Tell me . . . in detail.

Lao-hsin: (With a tone of weariness which suggests he realizes this conversation should have taken place two years before—that is, before Dogen became so proud of his intellect and debating skill.) When Ju-ching was a young monk he went to his abbot and asked if he could be put in charge of cleaning all the toilets in the monastery. Perhaps he thought that cleaning the toilets was the way to spiritual glory, or perhaps he sought to be "special" among the monks, or perhaps he hoped to win approval from the abbot, or perhaps for all of the above reasons. Whatever the reason at the time, it seemed like pious nonsense.

Dogen: What did the abbot do?

Lao-hsin: Threw him out, of course.

Dogen: Did the abbot say anything to the young monk?

Lao-hsin: Yes (as if trying to remember). The abbot said, "Before you clean the toilets, show me that which is never soiled."

Dogen: Wonderful, then what?

Lao-hsin: For two years the young Ju-ching worked on his abbot's question and then he returned to announce that he had at last experienced that which is never soiled. His abbot confirmed his insight and told Ju-ching: "Now you are fit to clean the toilets. So, find a shovel and get busy!"

Dogen: Take me to Ju-ching.

Lao-hsin: But your ship is in.

Dogen: Forget the ship. Please—take me to Ju-ching.

Lao-hsin: Well, he is not easy to meet. If he is not cleaning toilets, he is sitting in the *zendo*. He never leaves the *zendo* to visit his home. He does not speak with those who sit near him; he does not go to the rooms of the other monks.

Abbot though he is, he lives and eats with all the monks; he does not wear the robes of his office. He teaches the ignorant and, strangest of all, he welcomes non-Buddhists into his monastery and lets them live with the monks and nuns—this was until then, an unheard-of practice. He once refused an offer of ten thousand silver coins in exchange for a private talk with the local governor. Mostly he just sits. It is said his pants are worn out and the flesh of his buttocks has split open, but he continues to sit. All other abbots and teachers are in awe of him. Ju-ching advises them to sit and practice for he tells them, "Even if you have a little understanding, you must not become indolent, for if you do, you will lose what little insight you have . . ."

Dogen: (Begging) Please, take me to Ju-ching.

Lao-hsin: (Trying not to show his joy at realizing that bringing these two men, Ju-ching and Dogen, together will be without a doubt the greatest act of compassionate service he will ever perform for any man or woman.) Well, if you insist. (Consulting his calendar and thumbing the pages.) I suppose I can find the time to schedule it.

We know nothing of the meeting that must have taken place between Ju-ching and Dogen. We do know that Dogen was transformed from a proud and victorious debater into a humble and more deeply enlightened monk. Listen to him now, on his knees with his face to the floor, as he speaks to Ju-ching:

Though I sought the way from various masters and knew a little about cause and effect, I still did not know the Buddha Dharma. I was occupied with its names and forms. Now I, an insignificant person from a distant land, beg you in your great compassion, allow me to come to you day and night. Please teach me.[3]

The Zen gift of compassionate service flows from the insight one attains from practicing the earlier gifts which I have discussed. Living these gifts makes one wise and prepares one for the gift of compassionate service. Compassion without wisdom would be sentimental just as wisdom without compassion would be unthinkable. Who could reveal himself before a wisdom that was not tempered by compassionate love?

When I first went to Japan, I heard the Japanese Christians say that if we foreign Christians had sent contemplatives to them, they would have followed us anywhere. Of course they were impressed with our Christian schools and hospitals and orphanages, but they themselves had all these things in Japan. What they really wanted from us was something their culture has always treasured above all else. They were looking among us for someone like Ju-ching. They wanted a Ju-ching similar to the one to whom the local governor offered ten thousand silver pieces for a few moments in Ju-ching's presence and for his words of wisdom and compassion.

I have told you about Dogen, Lao-hsin, and especially Ju-ching to impress you with the reality that in the Zen tradition the accomplished human being does not sit home waiting to receive admirers. No, that human being is true to the most essential and fundamental Zen insight. My neighbor is my very self; my compassionate service to my neighbor can not be contrived. It must be as natural and as spontaneous as my breathing in and my breathing out.

To reinforce the Zen Buddhist understanding of compassionate service, I will refer to the work of the eminent Jewish theologian and philosopher Emmanuel Levinas.[4] In his writings Levinas argues that philosophy tends to pay too much attention to the nature of reality and the nature of language. He consequently tries to shift this emphasis to ethics. In his works Levinas contends that the main objective of valid philosophy is to teach us that instead of being distracted by unfeeling truths we, at every moment of our life, should subject ourselves to works of justice. For Levinas the main concern of thinking people should be the quality of their relationship to other people. To emphasize his belief he quotes the Lithuanian Rabbi Israel Saluter's memorable phrase, "The material needs of my neighbor are my spiritual needs."

Levinas differs from Martin Buber who in *I and Thou* concludes that the relationship between "I and thou" is reciprocal. For his part Levinas writes that the "I" should acknowledge the "you" as an irreducible person whether or not the "you" acknowledges the "I," simply because it is the "I"'s moral duty to do so, and the "I" must live according to this standard for which there is no outside justification. Levinas does not root his commitment to the other in his faith in God, but rather in his faith in God as God is manifested in the other. Relying on his early training in the Talmud, Levinas believes that we are justified in loving the Torah more than in loving God because we can only go to God by being ethically concerned for the other. To seek direct contact with God is for Levinas to cultivate madness because we can only go to God through our neighbor.

Writing about compassionate service to the other, Levinas is very close to the thinking of Simone Weil. Both Levinas and Weil write that attentiveness to the suffering face of the other is the core ethical principle of human life. Both concur that the epiphany of the afflicted face of the other constitutes my true self because that afflicted face interrupts me and impels me to seek justice for it and to seek it now. Their insight does not differ from the epiphanic insight of Douglas Roche, the former Canadian ambassador for peace to the United Nations who, while traveling for the U.N. in Bangladesh, visited a poverty-stricken village to see what help he could bring it. As he was leaving, he told me, a woman of the village rushed up to offer him a glass of date juice, a luxury she could scarcely afford. Recalling that moment, he told me, he had an unforgettable insight. He said he suddenly realized that the woman was his sister and that she and her children were starving. He said he asked himself, "What am I going to do about it?" It was this encounter with an "afflicted face" that turned Roche, while working in the United Nations, into a tireless seeker of justice for the poor.

We Christians believe Christ to be the messiah, the example par excellence of compassionate service. On this point Levinas agrees with the line of Jewish interpretation that interprets the concept of the messiah, the compassionate savior, as a parable describing what it means to be a true human rather than a real story revealing the destiny of a single individual. Levinas proposes that the messiah is no other than I myself, and to be myself is to be the messiah. When I do not avoid the burden imposed on me by the afflicted face of my neighbor, I am the messiah. This means I realize that in this life each of us is responsible for the other when the other appears before us in a unique and unrepeatable way. Believing and acting this way is for Levinas the true meaning of kenosis: that is, the continuous human emptying out of all limitations and clingings in order to be utterly transformed in the present moment. It means not looking back or forward in time to rely on the messianic act of another; it means standing up and being counted among the compassionate.

In his works Levinas sounds the same themes as those in the verse of the tenth ox-herding picture. His complete human being puts compassionate service to those in need before any abstract speculation about either the nature of things or the explanation of how we know them. The reality of the afflicted face breaks into our consciousness and demands a response from us. Levinas does not deny the existence of God but he reminds us that God can be only known and served when we attend to the material needs of our neighbor. This is a theme that every Christian should recognize: "Lord, when did we see you hungry?"(Matthew 25:44). Levinas's insistence that we are the messiah (we are Christ) and that the time for service is the present moment makes perfect sense to anyone in the Zen Buddhist tradition.

If you think the teaching of Levinas smacks of theory, let me put flesh and bones on it in the person of Etty Hillesum, a Jewish woman, who was swept up by the Germans in Holland in 1941 and sent to her death in Auschwitz in 1943. Though she knew nothing of Zen, her *Interrupted Life* parallels the final poem of our ox herder poet and puts a modern face on Zen teaching. In it she writes:

> And a camp needs a poet, one who experiences life there, even there, as a bard and is able to sing about it.

> At night, as I lay in the camp on my plank bed, surrounded by women and girls gently snoring, dreaming aloud, quietly sobbing and tossing, and turning, women and girls who often told me during the day, "We don't want to think, we don't want to feel, otherwise we are sure to go out of our minds," I was sometimes filled

with an infinite tenderness, and lay awake for hours . . . and I prayed, "Let me be the thinking heart of these barracks." And that is what I want to be again. The thinking heart of a whole concentration camp.[5]

To be the thinking heart of the barracks meant for Hillesum to turn from hatred to love. She writes:

I know that those who hate have good reasons to do so. But why should we always have to choose the cheapest and easiest way? It has been brought home forcibly to me here how every atom of hatred added to the world makes it an even more inhospitable place.[6]

In the end the departure for Auschwitz came suddenly, without warning. Hillesum writes that she with her father, mother, and brother firmly and calmly left Westerbork singing.[7]

In November 1999 I visited Auschwitz and Birkenau with a Peacemaker group from Europe and the United States led by Bernard Glassman Roshi. At Birkenau we visited a barrack that had been used to house women who, because they could no longer work, were waiting to be gassed and cremated. Since they were scheduled to die, they were not given food or water; and since the ovens could not cremate them fast enough, many women died of hunger and thirst on their plank beds. To remember these women and girls Jewish and Polish groups sang lullabies in the barrack and lit candles. As I watched and listened, my thoughts turned to Etty Hillesum who once may have been lying in the bunk I was standing beside, listening to sobbing in the night, attentive to every heartbreaking circumstance, refusing to give in to hate, and offering in her thoughts compassionate service to others.

What a wonderful modern version of the meaning of the tenth and final ox-herding picture—the ox herder's return to the marketplace. We observed that he was attentive and compassionate; and though his head was covered with ashes, his laughter streamed down his face. Etty Hillesum, a magnificent Jewish young woman, was indeed one with the ox herder. Clear-eyed, she refused to hate; and although she stepped into the worst life had to offer, she was the heart of the barrack, and went to her death singing.

Conclusion

In the second half of the twentieth century global communications have evolved to the point where the Christian world can no longer be ignorant of Zen Buddhism. The meeting of these two international religions can bring needed light and compassion to many. Their encounter must not be allowed to degenerate because of prejudgments and misunderstanding. Let us Christians then pay attention to the gifts that are offered to us, and gratefully accept and integrate into our lives all that is possible. And if we deem that there is some part of the gift we cannot understand or accept, then let us wait with hope for another generation of Christians to be able to integrate what we could not. In the meantime, in our conversations with gift-bearing teachers of other traditions, let us with Stephen Spender

> . . . think continually of those who were truly great.
>   . . . Whose lovely ambition
> Was that their lips, still touched with fire,
> Should tell of the Spirit, clothed from head to foot in song.[1]

Fortunately there is a new generosity and openness in the Christian world to non-Christian religions that can enrich us profoundly. The gifts Zen Buddhism offers cannot satisfy every personality and devotional orientation. Our scriptures and traditions will always completely nourish and develop many Christians. Yet there will be Christians who will be drawn to interfaith practice and will wish to enhance their faith with the Zen gifts depicted in these ox-herding pictures. The Zen Christian practice will not always be filled with light. We may experience that when we shift our devotional emphasis from the "last word" that has given us security and certitude, we will open ourselves to the possibility of doubt, pain, and loneliness. Recall the experience of Stephen Dunn who said that the sacred cannot be found unless we give up some old version of it; and when we do, we will experience an emptiness that will take a lifetime to fill.

Our reach must always extend beyond our grasp, and the mandate of the church to promote truths other than our own must be accepted and followed, for the goal is one of peace finally among religions.

Ponder once more the words of Denise Levertov:

> Imagine two neighboring hills, and
> your house, my house, looking across, friendly:
> imagine ourselves
> meeting each other
> bringing gifts, bringing news.[2]

Notes

Introduction

1. *Decrees of General Congregation 34* (Rome: Curia of the Superior General, 1995), 38.
2. Ibid.
3. Ibid., 43.
4. Ibid., 37.
5. *The Ox and His Herdsman: A Chinese Zen Text*, trans. M. H. Trevor (Tokyo: Hokuseido Press, 1969).
6. Denise Levertov, "Clouds," in *The Freeing of the Dust* (New York: New Dimensions, 1975), 63.

Chapter I. Practice

1. *The Ox and His Herdsman*, trans. M. H. Trevor, 6.
2. Francis H. Cook, *The Record of Transmitting the Light: Zen Master Keizan's Denkoroku* (Los Angeles: Center Publications, 1991), 221.
3. Hakuin Yasutani, *Flowers Fall: A Commentary on Dogen's Genjokoan*, trans. Paul Jaffee (Boston: Shambala, 1996), 72.
4. *The Zen Master Hakuin: Selected Writings*, trans. Philip B. Yampolsky (New York: Columbia University Press, 1971), 135.
5. Tom Stoppard, "Pragmatic Theatre," *New York Review of Books*, September 23, 1999, pp. 8–10.
6. Simone Weil, *Waiting for God* (New York: Harper & Row, 1992), 103, 109.
7. Joan Acocella, "Going Wild," *The New Yorker*, December 7, 1998, pp. 202–5.
8. George Eliot, *Daniel Deronda* (London: Penguin 1987), 296.
9. Ibid., 298.
10. Ibid.
11. Ibid., 299.
12. May Sarton, "9," in *Letters from Maine: New Poems* (New York: W.W. Norton & Company, 1984), 26.
13. Robert E. Kennedy, "Immortality in Oriental Religious Perspective," in *Human Life*, ed. William C. Bier, S.J. (New York: Fordham University Press, 1977), 270.

Chapter II. "Not Knowing"

1. *The Ox and His Herdsman*, trans. M. H. Trevor, 8.
2. Cook, *Transmitting the Light*, 58.
3. John P. Keenan, *The Mystery of Christ: A Mahayana Theology* (Maryknoll, N.Y.: Orbis Books, 1993), 102.
4. Gregory of Nyssa, *Patrologiae Graeca*, trans. J. Malherbe and Everett Ferguson (Mahwah, N.Y.: Paulist Press, 1978), cited in Keenan, *The Mystery of Christ*, 107.
5. Wislawa Szymborska, "The Poet and the World," in *Poems: New and Collected 1957–1997* (New York: Harcourt Brace & Co., 1998), xiv.
6. Ibid.
7. Szymborska, "Classifieds," 5.
8. Szymborska, "Utopia," 173.
9. Levertov, "Conversation in Moscow," 87.
10. Sandra M. Schneiders, "Contemporary Religious Life: Death or Transformation?" *Cross Currents*, Winter 1996–1997, p. 524.
11. Stephen Dunn, *Riffs and Reciprocities* (New York: W.W. Norton) cited in *The American Poetry Review* 27 (March/April 1998), 15.
12. *Striving Towards Being: The Letters of Thomas Merton and Czeslaw Milosz*, ed. Robert Faggen (New York: Farrar, Straus & Giroux, 1997), 38.
13. Ibid., 61.
14. Iris Murdoch, *The Green Knight* (New York: Penguin Books, 1995), 464.
15. Ibid.
16. Ibid., 95.
17. Ibid., 465.
18. Szymborska, "No Title Required," 225.
19. Joann Wolski Conn, *Horizons: The Journal of the College Theology Society* 26 no. 1 (Spring 1999), 157.
20. Willigis Jäger, *Search for the Meaning of Life* (Liguori, Mo.: Triumph Books), 20.
21. Denise Levertov, "Empty Hands," in *Sands in the Well* (New York: New Directions, 1996), 11.
22. Keenan, *The Mystery of Christ*, 103.
23. Szymborska, "Sky," 223.

Chapter III. Self-Reliance

1. *The Ox and His Herdsman*, trans. M. H. Trevor, 9.
2. *Two Zen Classics: The Blue Cliff Record; Hekiganroku*, trans. Katsuki Sekida (New York: Weatherhill, 1996), 166.
3. Ibid., 167.
4. *The Buddhist Bible*, ed. Dwight Goddard (Boston: Beacon Press, 1970), 87–102.
5. Mary Oliver, "White Flowers," in *New and Selected Poems* (Boston: Beacon Press, 1992), 59.
6. *Book of Serenity*, 206–9.

7. James Applewhite, "Prayer for My Son," in *River Writing* (Princeton, NJ: Princeton University Press, 1958), 119.

8. *Book of Serenity*, 176–79.

9. Oliver, "Rain," 3.

10. *Book of Serenity*, 176–79.

11. Ibid., 177.

12. Rita Dove, "Millennium Song," *New York Times*, December 25, 1999.

13. *Book of Serenity*, 167.

14. William Butler Yeats, "September 1913," in *Collected Poems* (London: MacMillan & Company, 1963), 120.

15. *The Gateless Gate (Mumonkan)*, trans. Koun Yamada (Los Angeles: Center Publications, 1979), 48.

16. Oliver, "Wild Geese," in *Dream Work* (New York: Grove/Atlantic, 1986), 110.

17. Ibid.

18. Homer, *The Odyssey*, trans. Robert Fagles (New York: Viking Penguin, 1996), 334.

19. Ibid., 419.

20. Ibid., 435.

21. Joseph Brodsky, "On Telemachus," in *A Book of Luminous Things*, ed. Czeslaw Milosz (New York: Harcourt, Brace & Co., 1996), 116.

22. Ibid.

Chapter IV. Impermanence

1. *The Ox and His Herdsman*, trans. M. H. Trevor, 12.

2. Rollo May, *Man's Search for Himself* (New York: W.W. Norton & Co., 1953), 115.

3. *The Gateless Gate*, 73.

4. *Book of Serenity*, 46–50.

5. Kathleen Raine, "This Body of Death," in *Collected Poems* (London: Hamish Hamilton, 1972), 159.

6. *The Gateless Gate*, 45–48.

7. Dale S. Wright, "Document of the Concept of Truth in Dogent Shobogenzo," *Journal of the American Academy of Religion* 54, no. 2 (Summer 1986), 273.

8. Raine, "The Pythoness," 95.

9. *Transmitting the Light*, 130.

10. Ronald Goodman, "The Four Houses," *The American Poetry Review* 28, no. 1 (January–February, 1999), 31–32.

11. Oliver, "One or Two Things," in *Dream Work*, 50.

12. Philomena Long, *American Zen Bones* (Los Angeles: Beyond Baroque, 1999), 103–4.

13. *No Author Better Served: The Correspondence of Samuel Beckett and Alan Schneider*, ed. Maurice Harmun (Cambridge: Harvard University Press), cited in Fintan O'Toole, *New York Review of Books*, January 20, 2000, pp. 43–45.

14. *The Poems of Robert Frost* (New York: Alfred A. Knopf, 1997), 101–2.

15. Ibid.

16. Rosemary Radford Ruether, "The unrealized promise of dialogue with Buddhism," *National Catholic Reporter,* June 4, 1999, p. 18.

17. John L. Allen Jr., "Vatican offers symbols of harmony," *National Catholic Reporter,* November 12, 1999, pp. 6–7.

18. Oliver, "Maybe," 97.

19. Ibid.

Chapter V. Self-Mastery

1. *The Ox and His Herdsman,* trans. M. H. Trevor, 13.

2. *The Blue Cliff Record,* in *Two Zen Classics,* 171–73.

3. Cook, *Transmitting the Light,* 118–20.

4. Anne Wroe, *Pilate: The Biography of an Invented Man* (London: Jonathan Cape) as reviewed by Brendan Walsh in *The Tablet,* January 4, 1999, p. 559.

5. Frank Kermode, *London Review of Books,* April 15, 1999, 17.

6. Cook, *Transmitting the Light,* 110–114.

7. Ibid., 114–119.

8. Ibid., 161–165.

9. Aileen Kelly review of "Chekhov the Subversive," *New York Review of Books,* November 7, 1997, 61–66.

10. Ibid.

11. Ibid.

12. Sandra Schneiders, "Contemporary Religious Life: Death or Transformation?" *Cross Currents,* Winter 1996–1997, 529.

13. *Lotus Moon: The Poetry of the Buddhist Nun Rengetsu,* trans. John Stevens (New York: Weatherhill, 1994).

14. Ibid.

15. Denise Levertov, "Annunciation in the House," in *A Door in the Hive* (New York: New Directions, 1989), 86.

Chapter VI. Incarnation

1. *The Ox and His Herdsman,* trans. M. H. Trevor, 15.

2. Cook, *Transmitting the Light,* 27–29.

3. Ibid., 29.

4. C.S. Lewis, *Letters to Malcolm: Chiefly on Prayer* (New York: Harcourt Brace & Co., 1983), 21.

5. *Book of Serenity,* 72–75.

6. Ibid., 74.

7. Kathleen Raine, "Advent," in *Living with Mystery: Poems 1987–1991* (Ipswich, U.K.: Golgonooza Press), 31.

8. *Book of Serenity,* 75.

9. Raine, "Seen in a Glass," 75.

10. Cook, *Transmitting the Light,* 194.

11. Ibid., 190–93.

12. Ibid., 193.

13. Emily Dickinson, "632," in *The Complete Poems*, ed. Thomas H. Jackson (Boston: Little Brown & Co., 1960), 312.

14. Raine, "Three Poems of Incarnation," 152.

15. Dickinson, "520," 254.

16. Andrew Louth, "The Wisdom of the Byzantine Church, Evagvios of Pontos and Maximos the Confessor," 1997 Paine Lecture in Religion, University of Missouri–Columbia, p. 18.

17. Thomas Fox, "Polite toward Rome, true to their mission," *National Catholic Reporter* 36, no. 13 (January 28, 2000), 10–11.

Chapter VII. Emptiness

1. *The Ox and His Herdsman*, trans. M. H. Trevor, 17–18.

2. "The Platform Sutra of the Sixth Patriarch: The Text of the Tun-Huang Manuscript," *Records of Civilization Sources Studies*, Hui-Neng Liu-Tsu-ta No. 76 (June 1978), 132.

3. Schneiders, "Contemporary Religious Life," 523.

4. David Toolan, "At Home in the Cosmos: The Poetics of Matter and Energy," *America*, February 24, 1996, p. 8.

5. Ibid.

6. Marie Ponsot, "Even," in *The Bird Catcher* (New York: Alfred A. Knopf, 1999), 84.

7. *Book of Serenity*, 183–186.

8. Cook, *Transmitting the Light*, 125.

9. *Book of Serenity*, 133.

10. Ibid.

11. Szymborska, "Nothing Twice," 20.

12. Szymborska, "An Effort," 8.

13. Francis Ferguson, "The Cherry Orchard: A Theatre Poem of the Suffering of Change," in *Anton Chekhov's Plays*, ed. and trans. Eugen K. Bristow (New York: W.W. Norton & Co., 1977), 382–95.

14. *The Gateless Gate*, in *Two Zen Classics*, 52.

15. *Blue Cliff Records*, 218.

16. Gerard Manley Hopkins, "Spring and Fall," in *Poems and Prose* (New York: Viking 1985), 50.

17. *Blue Cliff Records*, 266.

18. *The Gateless Gate*, in *Two Zen Classics*, 194–197.

19. Ibid., 197.

20. Keenan, *The Mystery of Christ*, 133.

21. Ibid., 133–37.

22. Oliver, "Orion," in *Dream Work* (New York: Atlantic Monthly Press, 1986), 49.

23. Ibid., "Robert Shumann," 23.

24. H. L. Mencken, *Chrestomathy* (New York: Vintage Books, 1982), 10.

Chapter VIII. No-God

1. *The Ox and His Herdsman*, trans. M. H. Trevor, 19.
2. Cook, *Transmitting the Light*, 62.
3. Ibid.
4. Ibid., 117.
5. Ibid., 122–23.
6. Ibid., 193.
7. Szymborska, "Psalm," 148.
8. Szymborska, "A Paleolithic Fertility Fetish," 102.
9. Szymborska, "View with a Grain of Sand," 185.
10. Cook, *Transmitting the Light*, 144.
11. Ibid., 186.
12. Ibid., 207.
13. Ibid., 215.
14. Denise Levertov, "Contraband," in *Evening Train* (New York: New Directions, 1992), 112.
15. Oliver, "First Snow," in *American Primitive*, 98.
16. Oliver, "Sunrise," in *Dream Work*, 59.
17. *Gateless Gate*, 242–46.

Chapter IX. No-Self

1. *The Ox and His Herdsman*, trans. M. H. Trevor, 21.
2. Cook, *Transmitting the Light*, 43–46.
3. Ibid., 46.
4. Daniel Berrigan, "No One Knows Whether Death, Which Men in Their Fear Call the Greatest Evil, May Not Be the Greatest Good," in *And the Risen Bread* (New York: Fordham University Press, 1998), 172.
5. Kabir, "What I Said to the Wanting Creatures," in *The Soul Is Here for Its Own Joy*, ed. Robert Bly (Hopewell, N.J.: Ecco Press, 1985), 73.
6. Simon Lays, *New York Review of Books*, April 18, 1996, 28–31.
7. Iris Murdoch, *The Good Apprentice* (New York: Penguin, 1987), 78.
8. Iris Murdoch, *The Green Knight* (New York: Penguin, 1993), 303.
9. Iris Murdoch, *A Fairly Honourable Defeat* (New York: Penguin, 1980), 233.
10. Peter J. Conradi, *Iris Murdoch: The Saint and the Artist* (New York: St. Martin's Press, 1986), 234.
11. *The Good Apprentice*, 205.
12. Richard Rohr, "Archetypal Priests Are Not Always the Ordained Priests," *America*, April 5, 1997, pp. 20–23.
13. Gerald Martin, "Changing Elements or People?" *America*, March 4, 2000, p. 22.
14. Donald Nicholls, *Triumphs of the Spirit in Russia* (London: Dalton, Longman & Todd, 1997), 194.

15. *The Zen Teachings of the Bodhidharma*, trans. Red Pine (San Francisco: North Point Press, 1987), 19.

16. Mary Oliver, "Blue Heron," in *White Pine: Poems and Prose* (New York: Harcourt Brace & Co., 1991), 20.

17. John Mc Kenna, "Eucharistic Presence: An Invitation to Dialogue," *Theological Studies* 60, no. 2 (June 1999), 294–317.

18. Oliver, "One or Two Things," in *Dream Work*, 50.

Chapter X. Compassionate Service

1. *The Ox and His Herdsman*, trans. M. H. Trevor, 23.

2. Cook, *The Record of Transmitting the Light*, 223–36.

3. Ibid., 230.

4. Robert Gibbs, "Emmanuel Levinas," in *The Post Modern God: A Theological Reader*, ed. Graham Ward (Oxford: Blackwell, 1977), 45–73.

5. Etty Hillesum, *An Interrupted Life: Diaries 1941–1943* (New York: Henry Holt Co., 1996), 225.

6. Ibid., 256.

7. Ibid., 360.

Conclusion

1. Stephen Spender, "The Truly Great," in *Selected Poems* (New York: Random House, N.Y., 1964), 19.

2. Denise Levertov, "Clouds," in *The Freeing of the Dust* (New York: New Dimensions, 1975), 63.

Also by Robert Kennedy, S.J.

Zen Spirit, Christian Spirit
The Place of Zen in Christian Life

"A fine blend of readable scholarship, personal reflection, and teaching. Kennedy, a Jesuit and Zen teacher (sensei) draws on his Christian traditions and years in Japan to give readers a memorable book."

—*Review for Religious*

"This book will be of particular interest to Christians who are both puzzled and intrigued by one who simultaneously professes Christian faith and engages in Zen practice. When Kennedy—a Jesuit, a practicing psychotherapist, and a Zen teacher—writes autobiographically, this book is at its best."

—*Booklist*

"This book deals with basic questions about Zen: What is it? How is it practiced? Is it compatible with Christianity?...At home with Master Hakuin and Master Gasan as he is with John Steinbeck and Edna O'Brien, Father Kennedy Sensei opens up two meditative traditions to savor their wisdom."

—*America*

"Kennedy shows other Christians a way of integrating Zen Buddhism and Christian belief. He does this convincingly and gracefully...by weaving together Zen poetry and poems, Western poetry and literature, scriptural texts and personal experience. He gathers his reflections into a structure that echoes the traditional stages of spiritual development: knowledge, love, purification and union."

—*National Catholic Reporter*